DANNY McGRAIN
in Sunshine or in Shadow

DANNY BOY

But come ye back
when summer's in the meadow
or when the valley's hushed and white with snow
'tis I'll be here in sunshine or in shadow
oh, Danny Boy, oh Danny boy
I love you so.

DANNY McGRAIN
in Sunshine or in Shadow

with

HUGH KEEVINS

Foreword by
KENNY DALGLISH

JOHN DONALD PUBLISHERS LTD
EDINBURGH

ISBN 0 85976 191 6

Our thanks to D.C. Thomson Ltd. for
permission to use the photographs printed
here and to Pat Woods for the precise
details of Danny McGrain's playing career.
Special thanks also to Kevin McCarra for
his vigilance in reading the text proofs.

Phototypeset by Newtext Composition Ltd.,
Glasgow. Printed in Great Britain by
Bell and Bain Ltd., Glasgow.

Foreword

I met Danny McGrain one morning in July, 1967, as arranged, in Argyle Street, Glasgow and travelled with him on a number 64 corporation bus to Celtic Park. It was our first day of training as full-time players with the club and since then I have accompanied Danny on much longer journeys than that one and can therefore say from experience that he is entitled to be spoken of in the same breath as the greatest full backs in the world.

His ability has, over the years, been matched only by his durability, because Danny has overcome physical problems that would have finished lesser men, and his natural tenacity has always shone through in his play for Celtic and Scotland.

It was never his way to dwell on these setbacks, and so it will be in the next phase of his life that follows his time with Celtic. Danny will let actions speak for him in a way that will be inspirational to those who work with him or only marvel from the sidelines.

By his doings on and off the field, Danny McGrain has always been an exemplary figure and he has achieved that status in a game where the good guys tend not to be the ones who are highlighted. The game has not heard the last of Danny McGrain, either, and that is our good fortune.

Kenny Dalglish

Introduction

On Monday, May 25, 1987, twenty years after the most famous day in Celtic's history, I walked into the banqueting hall of a hotel in Renfrewshire and seven hundred people stood up. They were not there to honour me but to pay homage to the European Cup-winning side of 1967, the Lisbon Lions. What I experienced, though, was a spontaneous outpouring of affection and gratitude from members of numerous Celtic Supporters' clubs who had appreciated watching me give of my best for the club over two decades. The walk to my table seemed to take forever as the room reverberated with their cheers, and the more I tried to get through the crowd attempting to shake my hand or slap me on the back, the further away it seemed to get. I was aware, too, of my wife, Laraine, who had been at my side for all of those twenty years, choking back the tears as we ceremonially made our way forward, more like an aspiring political candidate and his first lady than an ordinary married couple. The irony of that statement being, of course, that elevation to high office was the last thing I was in line for at Celtic Park.

The dinner was in recognition of eleven men who were immortalised in Portugal when they defeated Inter Milan, and it turned out to be only the start of a frantic week. The following Thursday David Hay became the first manager in Celtic's history to be formally sacked, and his place was taken by Billy McNeill, a figure genuinely entitled to the description of legend at the club. Before the week was out, Airdrie, another team with whom I had been very briefly associated, appointed a former Scotland teammate of mine, Gordon McQueen, as their new, full-time manager.

The only losers in all of this were David Hay and the man he had given a free transfer to without, I was told, consulting anyone else at Celtic Park, myself, Danny McGrain. It is best to begin my life's story, then, by ensuring that there are no misconceptions about where I stand today. I bear no grudge at all against David Hay in spite of what he did to me. If he felt I had done all I possibly could for Celtic, then that is fair enough, even though I would obviously beg to differ with that verdict. We have been through too much together as players with Celtic and Scotland for me to think ill of him on a personal level. It is also my understanding now that the manager did inform the directors I was going. What I do object to very strongly, then, is the manner in which I was discarded by Celtic, and within these pages I shall have my say on the question of the club and its supposed loyalty to the players who wear, or have worn, their hooped jersey. There will be some, possibly those who once played for Celtic or are devoted followers of the club, who will say it is wrong to air such private grievances in public and argue that it is not the Celtic way of doing things. I do not go along with that. It is only by highlighting Celtic's shortcomings that anything will ever get done within the club, as I know only too well from personal experience.

Since I was given a free transfer, there has also been a written dialogue conducted on the matter in the columns of every kind of newspaper, both tabloid and broadsheet. The most frequently aired criticism of myself is that, since I was given a testimonial match against Manchester United in 1980 by Celtic, I should be duly grateful and forget about being so greedy. First of all, I have never asked Celtic for a golden handshake in return for twenty years with the club and I have no intention of ever doing so. Let me make a couple of observations on that particular subject in passing, however.

In 1980, was I not entitled to a testimonial match after thirteen years with the same club, during which time I had fractured my skull and cost myself a year and a half's discomfort through a serious ankle injury while playing for them? Or is it nobler for a player to stay long enough with Celtic to make his name and then get himself a transfer, complete with the kind of massive signing-on fee that would probably be bigger than the sum I received after deductions?

In the final analysis Celtic did not give me a testimonial, in any case. A committee was formed of builders, lawyers, bookmakers and prominent supporters of the club to arrange various fund-raising activities, culminating in a game at Celtic Park. Out of the money raised, I paid Celtic for the use of the floodlighting, the hire of the stewards and the cost of the police bill, as well as sundry other expenses. I am not ungrateful to Celtic for the free hire of their ground, and this is not intended to be a spiteful reply to my critics, but the whole testimonial issue is irrelevant so far as I am concerned and, I would hope, the supporters who paid their money to get in because they wanted to be there.

To make myself perfectly clear, I don't want Celtic's money, but I could have used someone's time and thoughtfulness last May when I walked out of Celtic Park for the last time. A simple handshake and a word of thanks would have meant much more to me than a cheque made out to Danny McGrain. But no-one from the Celtic board of directors came near, and there was even worse to follow when the chairman, Jack McGinn, explained to me why that was the case, as the reader will discover.

Since the close season I have met with Jack McGinn and been taken out to dinner by him. He is a man I have respected for the amount of work he has done on Celtic's behalf, a labour of love since he obviously has a special devotion to the club, and I do not want anyone to think this book is all about the twenty minutes I spent inside Celtic Park on May 12, 1987, the day I went there for the last time.

It is not meant to be all about the selfish, uncaring Celtic Board of Directors, either. I can remember being given £1,000 by the late Chairman, Desmond White, in 1978 and told to take my family on a convalescent holiday to Majorca because I was having such difficulty in getting over a serious ankle injury. Like everything else in life, though, there are complimentary remarks a person can make about someone or something and critical comments that can be made as well. A football club, any football club, is no exception to that rule.

The faithful Celtic supporter will know what I am talking about, anyway. At the dinner for the Lisbon Lions, I was presented privately with a mounted golden boot bearing an inscription which read, 'Presented to Danny McGrain by the affiliation of registered Celtic Supporters' clubs in appreciation of an outstanding career'. That was all I wanted, a token of someone's respect. I should say that is the least I expected; the best I had hoped for was a job at Celtic Park. I know now that I was turned down by the board of the club on two separate occasions for a position on the staff there after my playing days were over. The first time was in 1986 shortly before the Celtic team of which I was captain won the Premier League Championship. The last refusal came just before I was released by the club. David Hay had gone to speak on my behalf for a post that would have seen me deal with the reserve-team players and was turned down flat. I have spoken to David Hay since his own dismissal from Celtic Park and had these facts verified. Because of that conversation, I know also that, while it was his decision to let me go, there might still have been a place for me at the club if anyone had shared his enthusiasm for the idea.

That they did not, and so obviously wanted me away from Celtic, is hard to accept, and even more difficult to understand. If I had been in control of the club and had wondered what to do with me after twenty years, the first thing that would have come to mind would have been to get some return on two decades' worth of wages. In that time Celtic had paid for my tuition under Jock Stein and Billy McNeill as well as getting me involved in further education through my sixty-two appearances for Scotland, working with men like Willie Ormond and Jim McLean. I would have wanted that depth of knowledge and experience kept at my disposal inside Celtic Park, even if a position had to be created for me. The directors were given two chances and didn't want to know.

I cannot conceal my disappointment over that state of affairs. It would not be possible to have played for Celtic for twenty years, and to have taken part in more games than anyone except two legendary figures of the club's almost one hundred year-old history, Jimmy McNair and Billy McNeill, and not care passionately about the club. My concern now, though, is for the players and Billy McNeill, not for those who run Celtic. I have been given ample cause over the years to take that uncomplimentary view of the directors, as will become apparent.

Anything that is said in a negative sense about Celtic is regarded as heresy by those who are fanatically devoted to the club, but they cannot be considered above criticism, and in appointing a new manager, for instance, the directors are reacting to what was sustained pressure on them to rediscover a sense of direction. It would be naive to assume, though, that just because Billy McNeill is back he will make everything better again. Rangers are still rebuilding and, in my opinion, they must start the season as favourites for all of the major domestic competitions. Anything Billy can get in Celtic's centenary year will only confirm his status as a god in the eyes of the supporters. What will happen to make a difference at Celtic Park, too, is that the players will know precisely what is expected of them. David Hay lost contact with his staff at the most fundamental level, through no fault of his own, because he was physically unable to take part in training sessions. His legacy from the days with Celtic and Chelsea was a knee that could not stand up to rigorous exercise.

Billy McNeill, even though he is forty-seven years old, will take part in practice matches and drive players remorselessly towards giving of their best for the thing he cares most about after his family.

He will be backed up by the tactical expertise of Tommy Craig. The swiftness and secrecy of David Hay's sacking was such that I was playing golf with Tommy at precisely the time the manager was being told by Jack McGinn his services were no longer required. It was only when Tommy drove back to the ground in the afternoon that he learned of the upheaval. I am glad he has been kept on, though, because he has a genuine contribution to make, being a highly respected coach who could have gone to Dundee United were it not for his high regard for Celtic.

I would like to think that the first step Billy and Tommy will take is to make sure the reserve players are brought back into a daily routine of training with the first team for the first time in four years. It has been the case recently that the two groups of players never worked together, and that always struck me as being particularly unhelpful to those who were brought into the first team at short notice. Whatever happens to Celtic now, however, they will not fail for lack of effort. I am only sorry I cannot be with them because forces inside Celtic Park, and I do not mean David Hay, were set against that idea for reasons that can only be guessed at.

Anybody looking in from the outside on the kind of summer I have spent might be wondering, in fact, if there is some hidden character defect holding me back, a flaw that has taken me from Celtic Park after twenty years without the offer of a job and then had me overlooked for a position at Airdrie which went ultimately in favour of a man who has not stayed in this country for fifteen years, Gordon McQueen. For the record, I do not gamble, I do not drink to excess and I am very happily married with three daughters, and if you can manage three girls, then I would have thought you could handle just about anything.

Why I did not get the job at Airdrie in 1986, when I was invited to go there by the most influential people at the club on the understanding that the board were unanimously in favour of me taking over, is not a source of mystery to me now, as I will explain later on. What does mystify me, though, is why, after rejecting me for the job and then losing the man who eventually got it, Derek Whiteford, within twelve months the Airdrie directors went off at a tangent to get Gordon. Billy McNeill had been their first choice during the close season, and that was understandable since he had only been in England a comparatively short time and also has a network of professional contacts here who were always going to help him re-adjust very quickly. With respect to Gordon McQueen, however, who was with me as a member of the Scotland World Cup squad in West Germany in 1974, what can he possibly know about the game in Scotland when he has spent fifteen years divided between Leeds United and Manchester United and his last working address was care of Hong Kong? I honestly wish him well, though.

Meanwhile, all that has happened to me only increases my determination to make my mark in this game at managerial level. In June I attended the S.F.A.'s management course at Largs as the first step towards gathering the qualifications I never had time to get as a player. It will always be my belief that practical knowledge of the game should not be overlooked either by those who are looking for men to run their clubs, and in twenty years with Celtic and Scotland I think I can safely lay claim to have seen and done most things. Good and bad, I have attempted to recall those experiences here, explicitly and without pulling out of making my opinion known if I think the subject demands plain speaking. Where I come from, that was the only kind of speech play we knew and, after all, this is basically the story of a Glasgow boy and a Glasgow football club, with special thanks to Jimmy Steele, Celtic's masseur, for keeping me on my feet for twenty years.

DANNY McGRAIN

Contents

1

From Schooldays to Pay-Days

For people like me, who were not particularly gifted at school and who had difficulty making faces, never mind anything with their hands, there were three kinds of job opportunities when you were born in Finnieston, in the centre of Glasgow, and then brought up in Drumchapel, on the outskirts of the city.

There was the road taken by someone like Billy Connolly, who came from the same streets, that led to the world of entertainment and allowed him to trade on his experiences and observations of Glasgow life.

For others, there was something a little less savoury, and a bit more risky, that operated on the fringes of legality and meant living on your wits. And then there was football.

When I left Celtic Park for the last time as a player after twenty years with that one club, I closed the door behind me at home and looked at a spacious villa, had the satisfaction of seeing children who were being privately educated and realised that, with a business of my own to fall back on, I had been fortunate enough to chance upon the one that had been absolutely right for me.

I would hope, too, that no-one resents me for what I have achieved because it took a lot of hard work to be able to take an inventory like that. The day I started to play the game for money was the day I stopped looking at football as a source of enjoyment and began to regard it as a job of work.

There can be no doubt that being a Celtic and Scotland player saved me from being just another statistic on the dole and introduced me to a lifestyle that I could otherwise never have hoped to enjoy, with its foreign travel and unforgettable memories of the people I met along the way, but I have only ever thought of myself as Danny McGrain, working man.

I am no different from any tradesman who ever served his apprenticeship, except that nobody comes to see them work or analyses their performance in the newspapers or on television.

My outlook could not have been shaped any other way coming from a family background that left no room for people with ideas above themselves or those who were not willing to give an honest

1

day's work for an honest day's pay.

I was born in Kelvindale Street, Glasgow, as the eldest of three sons, later moving round the corner to Grace Street, in Finnieston, on the banks of the Clyde.

My father, Robert, worked as an electrician until his retirement recently and if football ran in the family he was the one who started us all off. He had played for Hearts as a young man immediately after the war but a serious leg break brought a premature end to any aspirations towards making a living out of the game.

My mother, Margaret, like all the females who are truly the head of the family in Glasgow, had to put up with football being the main pre-occupation of the household but was fiercely supportive of her boys all the same.

It was an unremarkable upbringing, in as much as any of the families who survived such an environment fitted that description. The beginnings were the classically humble ones of an entire family housed in a room and kitchen with an outside toilet.

The McGrains, myself and my two brothers, Robert, who is now in New Zealand, and Tommy, never wanted for anything, though, and were always kept spotlessly clean, which couldn't have been easy since my only abiding memory of tenement life was of grimy buildings and streets with more people than seemed possible without developing claustrophobia living up an endless line of closes.

My earliest recollection of playing football, though, came when, in keeping with everyone else at that time, our family was decanted from the city centre and re-located in one of the new, sprawling housing schemes that were growing up in the Glasgow of the fifties.

Drumchapel was later to be summed up by Billy Connolly, after he had taken a good look at the place as a fellow resident, in two memorable phrases, the 'Desert wi windaes,' or the 'Cemetery wi' lights.'

It was the kind of place where the people called a balcony a verandah. The bath, the first one the vast majority of us had ever had in the house, was not always used solely for the purpose of bathing, either, being sometimes a makeshift washing machine for the larger families among us, although never, to my recollection, the impromptu coal scuttle of popular mythology. Not up our close at any rate!

The red light that signified the immersion heater working was admittedly mistaken by some on occasion as a danger signal that the equipment had overheated and quickly switched off again, but we all have to learn sometime.

We were called the Glasgow overspill, which sounds like someone's mistake, and in hindsight our parents were badly let down by whoever designed a place the size of a small town but forgot to put in it anything other than the usual endless rows of houses.

It was this oversight which was to bring about the gang warfare of my teenage years and although I kept as far away from it as was humanly possible I could understand and sympathise with the frustration of the kids involved, if not how they reacted to it.

While it was without doubt a planners' aberration, with no amenities like cinemas, play areas or clubs to act as diversions, Drumchapel was, for the very young like myself, a paradise, nevertheless. It was full of endless, green fields where you made your own entertainment by kicking a ball around from morning until night in games that had 'teams' of twenty or more a side and in which you were on the ball every quarter of an hour or so!

In the organised sense, my participation in the game began at Camus Place Primary School, although this introduction could hardly have been less auspicious.

The school had no pitch of its own, no team and, therefore, no strips, either. The lost tribe of Camus Place set about sorting that out with the help of a new head teacher, Mr. Johnstone, and that is how it came to be that in order to raise money for his first proper football jersey the eight-year-old Danny McGrain made wicker baskets along with the rest of the boys in the class and then sold them around the doors of the neighbourhood.

Anyone in Drumchapel who still has one of those as an heirloom, incidentally, will now know what I meant when I mentioned being useless with my hands!

We were eventually kitted out in strips of blue horizontal stripes and took to playing in the local school league, with every match being played away from home. Nomads we might have been but at least we looked the part.

The football disease was confirmed in my blood by then, too, and there was no sacrifice too great to get on. By the time I was old enough to move on to Kingsridge Secondary School, in fact, I had taken on a milk run to buy myself my first decent pair of boots. It meant getting up at four o'clock in the morning and coming back into the house in time to change for school, and all for the princely sum of thirty shillings a week with the same amount of predecimalised money in tips. What with that, lessons and playing football after four o'clock, at least I had no time to notice there was nothing else to do in Drumchapel.

It was also about this time that I began to realise that football was doing something else for me. I had no self-confidence in the classroom – I was the pupil who always took the seat at the back of the room and kept his mouth shut for fear of giving the game away – but on the football pitch I found I was able to express myself, to show off the skills I had been acquiring.

It was where I was at my boldest, apart from the day I asked out one of the girls in my year, Laraine Dunaby, who, thankfully, recognised someone in need of a bit of help off the field and is still assisting to the present day as Mrs. McGrain.

On the park I was able to help myself to the extent that I was chosen for the Glasgow schools team, playing against London at Hampden Park, which gave me a taste for pursuing my ambition as far as I could. It might never have been Danny McGrain of Celtic, in fact, because at the age of sixteen West Bromwich Albion asked me to go down to the Midlands on trial with them.

My father, though, advised me against it because there was a rule at that time which debarred any boy who had been on approval with a senior club from representing his school at international level. He thought going to the Hawthorns, and possibly failing, was too much like putting all my eggs in one basket.

The irony of the situation is that the road which ultimately led to Celtic Park for me was therefore built by a man who was then a devoted Rangers supporter. My father had taken me with him to Ibrox as a boy when Rangers had their fine team of the early sixties with players like Jim Baxter, who was my first hero, Davie Wilson and Willie Henderson.

In hindsight, I suppose his dearest wish then would have been for me to sign for Rangers, and to this day I believe that I would have done, too, but for their sectarian policy that made an Ibrox scout run a mile in the opposite direction when he heard my full name was Daniel Fergus McGrain and assumed, mistakenly, that I was a Catholic.

The story was told to me by someone at Queens Park when I was playing for their Victoria XI, and even twenty years later I still find it distasteful and frustrating that, as a people, we can still be this divided in Scotland. Daniel Fergus McGrain was my grandfather's name and is commonplace throughout the various branches of my family. It is not Irish-Catholic, as everyone seems to think, but dates back to my forefathers on the Isle of Skye.

I am not very happy that I should even have to explain that in print because I cannot stand religious intolerance of any kind. Even as a child when some of those around me took to indulging in the old, tribal rituals of asking other youngsters if they were a 'Billy, a Dan or an old tin can,' in order to establish their religious denomination, and then thumped those who did not pass the theology test, I wanted no part of it. I still don't.

It seems to me that these energies could be spent far more productively, although the religious divide has, admittedly, given me cause to smile over the years that I was known as the Protestant captain of the so-called Catholic club. I remember once, for instance, taking my seat in the stand at Hampden before an international match there and being spotted by one of the religious zealots.

Overcome with rage at the very sight of me for some reason, he started to shout, 'McGrain, ya Fenian B------' when the words froze on his lips because of their obvious unsuitability. In the end, after searching what there was of his brain, he came up with a frenzied 'McGrain, ya diabetic B------!' Presumably, if you could see diabetes, from which I suffer, if would be green and white in colour and deeply offensive to Rangers supporters.

On a less humorous note, though, I regret to say that I still very much doubt if Rangers' policy of not signing Catholic players, no matter how good they are, will change in my lifetime. There is a new regime at Ibrox and the suspicion is that the ways of the last century and more will change but I think that Rangers' hands are tied because the majority of their supporters want the club to stay the way it is and could not accept a Catholic playing in the first team.

And while Rangers are as successful as they have been so far under Graeme Souness, who is married to a Catholic and does not, I know from personal experience, hold any bigoted views on the subject of religion, I think that is all the more reason to suspect the subject will fade from prominence as a topic for discussion.

The Ibrox policy is too deep rooted and there is too much at stake for them now to do anything about it. It would cost Rangers revenue and that is why, in spite of assurances that the barriers would come down, there has never been a Catholic signed in modern times. I don't honestly think I would like to become the token Catholic player at Ibrox, in any case, because it would be the definition of the no win situation.

If he was good he would still get abused by a section of the Rangers support and if he struggled to establish himself the same people would accuse him of not trying a leg.

The fact of the matter is I was never given the opportunity to get inside Ibrox and find out for myself what goes on there because asking a player what his name is can still be a loaded question where Rangers are concerned.

The devastation I felt over that episode quickly gave way to the more basic emotion of fearing what I was going to do with myself for the rest of my working life, which was just about to start.

For the record, and just to prove that I went to school morning and afternoon as well as playing football for Kingsridge, I shall now reveal the full extent of the scholastic qualifications as attained by Danny McGrain. These comprise 'O' levels in English, which has been handy for conversations with Kenny Dalglish over the years, Mathematics, invaluable for working out goal difference in the league table, Arithmetic, even handier for counting the takings at my pub near Parkhead, and Technical Drawing, which very nearly led me into a career move that would almost have been as inadvisable as staying on for my highers.

When, in desperation, I applied for a place at college to train as a mechanical engineer, I have to confess that I didn't really know what the term meant. I'm not sure that I do to this day. There was no interest being shown in me by any professional club, though, so I resigned myself to the fact that I would play one, last international match for Scotland schoolboys and then accept that a career in football was simply not to be.

The game was against England at Ibrox of all places and much as I was intent on enjoying the experience to the full, convinced that it would be the last of its kind, there was so much that went wrong there was hardly anything right about the moment.

I was immediately struck by the size and speed of the boys from England, who looked like nobody I had gone to school with. In those days I played left half, what would now be termed the left-hand side of the midfield, but I left the pitch feeling I hadn't given a good enough account of myself while chasing those lithe giants around the park.

It didn't help matters, either, that I had to be helped off at the final whistle suffering from the effects of cramp. The greatest source of pain and frustration, however, was the score itself, a resounding 4-1 win for England. This was not the stuff of which memories were supposed to be made, yet it still turned out to be the turning point in my life.

It was only after I had been with Celtic for a year, in fact, that I discovered there was a man sitting in the stand at Ibrox that night I had never met before by the name of Tommy Reilly. He was a longstanding personal friend of Sean Fallon, then the assistant manager at Parkhead and one of the finest people it has been my good fortune to meet in football.

A couple of days after the match Sean telephoned our house in Drumchapel and said he wanted to come to discuss the possibility of signing me for Celtic. I can honestly say now that, in spite of coming from a family whose leanings had been more towards Rangers' side of Glasgow, there was never the slightest hesitation on my part that I would, given the chance, leap at going to Parkhead. This was the club, after all, who had just become the most successful in Britain by winning every domestic trophy as well as being the toast of Europe for the style they showed by winning the Champions Cup from Inter Milan in Lisbon.

There were certainly no misgivings on my mother's part. If my memory serves me correctly she was actually giving our close in Airgold Drive a thorough scrub down, the highest mark of respect a Glaswegian can pay an honoured guest, when Sean Fallon arrived. He was then given a personal escort to the flat on the top landing, just in case there were any tragic errors and he left without having done what he had set out to do. The negotiations may have been the quickest in the history of footballers' contracts, and it was agreed that I would formally sign for Celtic at Parkhead the following Sunday.

In recognition of the solemnity of the occasion it was decided that I could not go there by corporation bus, which would normally have been the case, and that is how Danny McGrain came to be driven to the famous old building in the East End of Glasgow by the same milkman who had given me the job that bought me my first proper boots. Not on the milk float, I hasten to add!

If the signing ceremony, which was conducted in an empty ground, was the fulfilment of an ambition, there was a privately concealed twinge of regret when Celtic, through Sean, told me that I could not, as I had hoped, go on to the ground staff as an apprentice professional straight away.

Instead, Celtic wanted me to keep up my training for a job outside football, which I had just begun at the Reid Kerr College in Paisley.

My instructors there might have been able to convince Celtic that was not such a good idea. There can rarely have been a more dangerous specimen in front of a lathe than myself, although half of the time I could not have been properly wakened up.

My prospects of becoming a time-served mechanical engineer were about as remote as the college was from my house. In order to get there it took three buses as well as a ferry trip across the Clyde where it separates Clydebank from Renfrew. On the nights that I trained at Parkhead with the other young boys in my position, there was a danger of developing travel sickness before I got as far as the ground.

For a growing boy it was a rigorous lifestyle, hard on the muscles to the extent that there were times when I risked embarrassment by standing all the way home on a half-empty bus because I was too sore to sit down. It was also torment for the mind, wondering if I was going to be taken on as a full-time player by the club. At the time I was getting five pounds a week from Celtic in expenses, but all I could think about was signing for them. Anyway, that's my excuse for the time I set the family home on fire.

Even budding Celtic players were still expected to make the tea if they were home before their mother and father. What they were not supposed to do was give their younger brother a chess lesson at the same time while a frying pan exploded into flames in the kitchen.

It was panic under pressure of a type I can never remember afflicting me on the field in later years as I frantically pushed Robert out the front door, dialled the emergency service on 999 and then hung up without giving the fire brigade any directions to the house.

Clearly, this distracted way of living could not go on, if only for the sake of life and limb, so the relief was overwhelming when Celtic finally agreed to let me give up my apprenticeship at college and become a full-time player at Parkhead.

When I think back on those days now, I genuinely thought I would be deposing the players who were then in the first team within weeks of arriving at the place. The incredible excitement surrounding Celtic's achievements was still able to be reached out to and touched, and yet I was going to remove the Lisbon Lions from their den!

My instinctive reaction on being called up, in fact, was that I had, as they say on the streets of my native Glasgow, cracked it. I had been saved from a life of manual labour and dropped into an adulation-filled existence where success was guaranteed. I knew it all.

There was, though, lurking in the background a man I had yet to meet, someone who was going to show me that what I really knew about the game then you could have written down on the back of my first national insurance stamp at Parkhead and still found room to lick it.

He would instil in me the good habits that would sustain me throughout the next twenty years of my life and tell me that the first of those revolved around everything being based on hard work.

His name was Jock Stein.

2
Jock Stein

The night Scotland played Wales at Ninian Park in Cardiff, I was no different from a high percentage of the population, sitting at home and watching the match with a knot in my stomach that would only be untied in the event of the team I had captained in the previous World Cup qualifying for their fourth successive finals. It was the tenth of September, 1985, and looking back on it now I should have realised there was something seriously wrong at the time.

Where I differed from the rest of the television-watching public was that I had looked over at the dug-out literally hundreds of times to see Jock Stein's expression during a match, but I can never recall the big man looking as distant as he did that night. Even when Davie Cooper scored from that penalty kick to take Scotland through to a play-off against Australia and eventually to Mexico for the finals themselves, Jock Stein looked remote, set apart from the excitement that was going on all around him.

When the television cameras then pictured him being carried into the dressing room I began to realise there was something horribly wrong that nobody had noticed because they were pre-occupied with the all-important result. I sat where I was, not wanting to telephone, or speak to, anybody. After the television news flash brought confirmation of his death, caused by heart failure, I went straight to bed.

Even in the morning I could not accept that he was gone. From the age of seventeen, when I met Jock Stein on my first day as a full-time player with Celtic, my impression of him was that the man appeared indestructible. In 1973 he had survived heart trouble and came back to pick up as if he had never left off at his beloved Celtic Park. Two years after that his sheer physical strength had enabled him to withstand a horrific car crash, which left him clinging on to life for two weeks in a hospital near Dumfries.

My only consolation as I went through the motions during the days leading up to his funeral was that I genuinely believed Jock Stein had gone the way he would have wanted to go, and that still does not strike me as a stupid or insensitive thing to say. His life really did revolve around the game of football in a way I have never detected in anyone else and I could not think of a more fitting end than a moment of triumph on the field of play.

At the funeral service in Linn Crematorium on the outskirts of Glasgow, I suddenly found it all very hard to take, however. The big man, as those closest to him knew, was everywhere. Without being disrespectful, I half expected to hear his voice and it was only when I saw his coffin that I became emotionally affected in a way I had never experienced before.

Part of me wanted to shout out for the service to be stopped, and as I made my way home that day afterwards, a dark and rainy Friday as I recall, I also felt sorry that he had been cremated. Jock Stein was such an important figure to so many people, from the players he worked with to the supporters who idolised him, that I felt a sense of frustration he did not get buried instead. Then there could have been a shrine where the public could have gone to pay their respects.

They took the only chance they could get the day after his funeral when a crowd of 39,450 turned out at Celtic Park to watch Celtic play Aberdeen and to chant his name at the place where he became a legendary figure and put one football club, as well as the city it came from, on the map. I don't think it would be unreasonable to ask here why the Glasgow City Fathers never formally recognised Jock Stein after his death. A monument to him in George Square, the biggest landmark, would not have been asking too much, in my opinion, since he was respected by football followers of all persuasions and by others who just became mesmerised by his abundant common sense.

It was ironic Celtic should have been playing Aberdeen that weekend of all times, too, because in Alex Ferguson, who was then their manager, I see the closest likeness of Jock Stein's image. They shared the same slavish devotion to the game, respected proper attention to duty and had identically fertile imaginations when it came to tactics and playing the game with flair. Alex looked unconcerned that afternoon, too, even though his team had just lost, which told me that his mind was not on the game at all but was taking him back to that bench at Ninian Park, where he had sat beside the most important man in the history of Scottish football throughout the last minutes of his life.

I don't think that description of Jock Stein is in any way an exaggeration, and I'll go further. In the almost one hundred-year existence of Celtic Football Club there has never been a more influential figure and the contribution he made at Celtic Park has never been adequately recognised in all the time that has elapsed since he passed away.

All the club have done is to hang up a photograph of Jock Stein inside a display cabinet that adorns the foyer of the pavilion at Celtic Park when the least they could have done was to re-name the stand, or even the ground itself, after the man who should never have been allowed to leave there in the first place.

When Jock Stein was offered a post as a director with special responsibilities for Celtic Pools in May 1978, eleven years to the day after he had made them the first British team to win the European Cup, I knew then he would not stay long at the club. If ever a man needed close involvement with players it was him, and although Billy McNeill was coming from Aberdeen to manage the club, there should have been a position created for Jock Stein in the way that Liverpool used, and still use, Bob Paisley as a consultant.

It need not mean getting in the way of the younger one in charge. Billy McNeill was the only man who could have followed someone like Jock Stein and he made an outstanding job of it at Celtic Park before he, too, was unceremoniously offloaded before being in turn reinstated, but if I had been the one coming to the club I would have insisted on the big man staying. How anyone could knowingly cast aside that depth of experience and wisdom is totally beyond me. To some extent, Celtic still live on the aura that Jock Stein created around them, but when he eventually left for Leeds United on a short-term basis before taking over the Scotland side a lot of spirit at the ground went out the front door with him.

There have been widespread suggestions that Jock Stein left Celtic Park for reasons completely unconnected with the game itself. So far as I am concerned these stories are unsubstantiated and it is up to individuals to draw their own conclusions about that. All I know is that he was irreplaceable and the best thing that ever happened to Celtic. I know they speak of Jimmy McGrory, who was still at the club in an administrative capacity when I joined in 1967, for his goalscoring exploits. Willie Maley, who devoted over fifty years of his life to serving Celtic as both player, manager and official is another prominent figure in the club's history, but no-one will ever mean more to me than Jock Stein.

My only regret is that I was not at the ground on the day he left so that I could have thanked him properly for all he had done to give me a career in the game. At the time I was trying to get over a mysterious ankle injury that had already cost me a year out of football, and which I will deal with at greater length later on.

A few days after he had gone to Leeds, though, the telephone rang at home one night and it was Jock Stein. He thanked me for all my efforts over the years, wished me well with my recovery and gave me his private telephone number which I was to call if ever I needed help or advice. I hung up and sat back down, thinking about the first time I had ever set eyes on Jock Stein.

It was in July, 1967. Kenny Dalglish and myself had gone to see him after Celtic's Under 18 Youth team, of which we had both been a part, came back from a tournament at Casale Monferrato in Italy. That was the first time I had ever been on an aeroplane or gone abroad and although we slept six to a room, as I remember, in what was more of a hostel than a hotel, the thirst for more of the big-time atmosphere was unquenchable.

I still had three years left to do of my apprenticeship at College, which seemed like a life sentence the way I was steadily deteriorating there, and Kenny was equally unhappy as an apprentice joiner. We both asked Jock if we could go on to the ground staff and to our extreme delight he agreed. That was the easy part. In all the years I knew him, I lived in awe of Jock Stein and it started that scorching hot day Celtic began training in preparation for the new, 1967-68 season. In those days the first-team players and the reserves trained together, but it was not the shock of working beside the European Cup-winninig side, the Lions of Lisbon, that put me off. A psychiatrist might have an explanation for it, saying it was all in the mind, but the first time Jock Stein came over to supervise my group I immediately developed cramp doing a hurdles exercise and knocked over every one of them like a car suddenly out of control with a burst tyre.

He just looked at me and said, 'In you go, wee man,' pointing to the dressing rooms. I know it was first-day fright since cramp ought not to happen to normal, fit boys of seventeen and because the following day I was perfectly all right.

Far from having a debilitating effect on me, I would say it was thanks only to Jock Stein that I had twenty years at the top of my profession. There are so many youngsters today who are introduced to the game at its highest level before they are really ready and who are, consequently, burned out before they know it, losing years off the other end of their careers. Jock Stein knew how to let someone emerge gradually at Celtic Park and it was a rarity to find a teenager in one of his teams.

What he did do for you, though, was to make sure that you

learned so much from him you were two years further advanced than people your own age with other clubs. At the end of our first season together, a reserve side that was made up of people like David Hay, Kenny Dalglish, Lou Macari, George Connolly and myself was actually good enough for Jock to go to the Scottish League Management Committee and ask if he could put Celtic's second team into the old-style Second Division. The request was thrown out in a matter of days, even though there were an uneven number of nineteen teams in that league and the interest created at the turnstiles could only have been good news all round.

I still believe the fear was that Celtic had so many good players we would have won the league. It had already been made part of the club's proposal, though, that we would not expect promotion in the event of that happening. The reserves, in fact, would have become steadily weaker because, one by one, Jock would have plucked us out of there and put us in the first team. The Scottish League would have none of it, though, and so we continued our education under the man who, I believe, introduced tactics to the Scottish game. Having said that, anywhere would have been better than the place Celtic sent me to further my training after I had signed for them.

Let me start by saying that the people who ran and played for Maryhill Juniors could not have been any friendlier or more helpful while I was with them. Maryhill were chosen because they were the nearest junior club to my home in Drumchapel, but they were the furthest thing from my mind when I thought about organised football. There is no quicker way to summarise my six months with Maryhill than to say the team never won a single game in all that time!

Junior football was then the preserve of players who had once been seniors but were now padding out time or those who were enthusiastic but unable to operate at a higher level. In my stay there I don't believe I learned one, single thing about the game itself but I did absorb a few lessons that would improve my attitude.

The experience taught me what it was like to be a loser and made me more determined not to feel that way again if I could possibly help it. In later years I would also learn to fully appreciate the value of a win, but understand that it was something to be celebrated over only on the day it happened. The next day you got down to work again trying to avoid being a loser.

I still have one memento of my days with Maryhill, too, and that is my award for being their Player of the Year. It sits in my house beside international caps and medals in recognition of wins in the League Championship, the League Cup and the Scottish Cup and I would not part with it even though, whenever I think of my junior days, I have this mental image of my team-mates sitting in the dressing room at half-time with a can of lager by their side and a cigarette on the go.

There would be none of that at Celtic Park, of course, as I found out when I was brought back from Maryhill into the real world. Jock Stein detested over-indulgence where drink was concerned and I never touched a drop until three years after he left Celtic Park for the last time, by which time I was thirty years old. Jock was a strict disciplinarian who had an intelligence network throughout Glasgow on a scale that would have made certain government agencies envious.

He could not only tell you where you had been the night before, but who you were with, and I have seen players who were invited into his private office for a more intimate meeting about such matters come out looking a distressing colour. It is often said of him, in fact, that Jock might have driven some people to misbehaviour because he would treat the Celtic team, even the most experienced and successful of them, like so many schoolchildren.

I believe he was a superb psychologist, who knew who he could abuse and who needed to be coaxed. If I had been bawled out by him as a youngster over anything at all, I know I could not have taken it, so the day I witnessed big Jock give Billy McNeill and Jimmy Johnstone, two of Celtic's most revered players, a tongue lashing I made up my mind that the manager would have an attentive and well-behaved pupil in Danny McGrain. It was only when I was old enough to be told the truth that Billy and Jimmy explained that Jock had meant the whole exercise to have that effect on me.

It was not that Jock ever used torrents of bad language, either. He just made you feel so small and inadequate that you could not wait to get out on the ground and train so that the vast stadium would swallow you up. He would always wait outside the dressing-room door, however, to drape one of those big arms around your shoulder and kill any ill feeling with a few conciliatory words. What was said in the dressing room by way of criticism was never to be forgotten but it was also over and done with so far as he was concerned.

Jock was too busy instructing to have time for petty distractions. To my mind he became so famous in the early sixties because he was like an inventor who noticed a gap in the market for a commodity he could provide. Nobody thought about the geometry of the game the way he did. As a manager he took the blinkers off those under him and taught them to think about the whole field and not just the little bit they played in. It was revolutionary thinking at a time when full backs, like myself, were popularly thought to be only good for winning the ball and then seeing how far they could kick it from one end of the park to the other.

The debt the game in this country owes to Jock Stein is therefore immense. He influenced a coming generation of men like Alex Ferguson, Jim McLean and Billy McNeill and they helped, as managers, to bring about a more competitive league that has retained the interest of the spectating public. What kind of state would our national game be in now had it not been for the unlikely leadership, and imagination, of a big miner from Bellshill?

It was only through a process of elimination under Jock that I became a full back. I had played in midfield and even at centre half for Celtic's reserve side before he found out what I did best and got me to play to my strengths.

At the end of that first full season with Celtic I then found out about another side of him, Jock Stein, the paymaster general. I had been getting by, just, on a very small wage with the club of twenty-eight pounds. It was so puny I had to supplement my income with the money I had saved in the bank from my time as a milk-boy in Drumchapel. When I went, sheepishly, to discuss a new contract with Jock Stein I made up my mind to be brave and not accept a penny under forty pounds a week. He offered me eighty-five pounds and I was so shocked I almost asked if that was to be shared among the entire reserve team.

Jock knew what was fair where the younger ones were concerned. It was only in later years, when I knew what I really wanted, that I came out beaten down by the manager to the figure he wanted to pay me.

Big Jock looked after me well, though, even after he had gone from Celtic. He was one of the organising committee who arranged my testimonial match against Manchester United at Celtic Park in 1980. By then I had known the man for thirteen years but it was only that night, Monday, the fourth of August, that I did something to him I had never done before. At the post-match dinner in a Glasgow hotel I presented him with a special gift, and when I asked him to come forward to receive it that was the first time in my life I had ever called Jock by his first name!

Even when I was in my second full season with Celtic I never had the nerve to call him so much as boss. That title, I felt, belonged only to those who had really been through it all with him, the European Cup team. To me he was 'Mr. Stein' and that was as familiar as I would get for a long time to come. There were plenty of occasions when I wanted to march up to his door and be a bit more adventurous by asking him when I was ever going to get into his first team, but I never did, and for that I have to thank Willie Fernie. He was then helping coach the reserve team, and whenever he noticed I was becoming despondent Willie would reassure me that I had the ability to break through one day and that all I had to do in the meantime was keep on working hard.

Just when I was beginning to doubt even Willie's word, the name of Danny McGrain appeared at last on Celtic's team sheet for the first time on Wednesday, the 26th of August 1970 as a substitute against Dundee United in a League Cup tie at Tannadice. As it turned out, my debut was forced upon me in regrettable circumstances. At half-time in the match, Harry Hood was told of an illness in his family that meant he had to leave immediately for Glasgow.

I remember that big Jock never said very much to me after telling me to get ready. He told me later on that was because he knew I was over-excited and would instantly forget everything he had said, in any case. He would have been absolutely correct, too.

Even though there was a crowd of 16,000 inside Tannadice that night, I never heard a sound, not even when the ball came to me for the first time and I let it slip under my foot and out for a throw-in. The manager must have thought he had signed an idiot.

Gradually, though, I came round and in the weeks that followed I held on to my place in the first team, including my baptism in the Old Firm game which Celtic won at home. My confidence was good, too, but that was mainly because I was being nursed along by the survivors of the Lisbon Lions, and if you couldn't play the game in the company of people like Bobby Murdoch, Billy McNeill, John Clark and Jimmy Johnstone, then you just couldn't play, it was as simple as that.

My promotion was short-lived, however, because Jock always knew instinctively when a youngster was due a rest again. Perhaps the greatest pity of all was that he was not as particular about recharging his own batteries. The big man allowed himself to rest for only twelve days after his first brush with heart trouble and when, two years later, he fought back after the car crash that almost cost him his life he was still doggedly fighting to overcome a change in his own personality.

It was clear to me from the day he walked back inside Celtic Park that this was not the Jock Stein I knew. He tried to rekindle his own enthusiasm by signing a succession of players from smaller clubs, attempting to play the transfer market as spectacularly as he had done years before when he was able to bring men like Joe McBride and Willie Wallace to Celtic for a song. The imaginative ideas that came off a decade before were no longer working, though, and the sale of Kenny Dalglish to Liverpool in 1977 was the last, dispiriting straw on top of the loss of Alfie Conn and Pat Stanton to the game through injury.

Celtic finished Jock Stein's last season in charge by only reaching fifth place in the Premier Division and losing in the final of the League Cup to Rangers. There was also the humiliation of being knocked out of the Scottish Cup by Kilmarnock, from the First Division, after a replay.

Moves went on behind the scenes, and instead of being properly thanked for all he had done for Celtic Jock Stein was let go after a testimonial match in his honour, his managerial powers having been assumed to have diminished from the moment of impact during a head-on collision on the notorious A74, near Lockerbie, in July, 1975.

That was not an opinion shared by the S.F.A., though, and Jock Stein proved in seven years as manager of Scotland that all he was looking for was a subtle change of pace. What a pity Celtic never realised the same thing or that marvellous brain could have been working on their behalf instead of the national side's.

It is now my dearest wish to go into club management for the first time at the same stage in life, my late thirties, that Jock Stein did when he took over Dunfermline and began to write his own remarkable story. I have no desire to be a Jock Stein clone, rather to help point people in the right direction by combining my own ideas with his influence.

In other words, the lessons that I really began to pick up when Jock had to dismantle the most famous side in Celtic's history and start all over again.

3

Highlights . . . and No Lights!

The young players that Jock Stein had gathered around him at Celtic Park had all been put on standby to form the new backbone of the team since May, 1970 when the club lost its second appearance in a European Cup final, this time against Feyenoord of Holland. It took place, ironically, in the city of Milan, the very name of which had been synonymous with triumph and not disaster up until then.

It was obvious to those of us still new to the game, who had been taken along to watch and learn from the preparation for the occasion at the San Siro Stadium, that the manager was mentally constructing the dismantling of the Lisbon Lions and the rebuilding of Celtic on the flight home from Italy. Within a year the European Cup-winning side of 1967 would play together for the last time in a league match, against Clyde at Celtic Park, honoured by the attendance of 35,000 people. Retirement came the way of Ronnie Simpson and there would be transfers for Bertie Auld and John Clark to begin the process of natural wastage.

In and around these happenings I made my first-team debut, but anyone attempting to keep pace with the story thereafter would have needed shorthand. Within the space of two years I played in every domestic competition for Celtic, received my baptism in Europe, got married, fractured my skull, made a complete recovery and then, after just two games for Scotland's Under 23 side, got my first full cap for my country. The rest of the time was my own.

In any considered analysis of that period in my career the starting-off point would have to be an appreciation of how much the Lisbon Lions meant to those of us at Celtic Park who were still young enough to share the same razor blade in the dressing room. Here were a collection of diverse personalities who had created a legend in their own lifetime yet were not, either individually or collectively, too big to pass on any advice to the greenest member of the groundstaff.

There were no bills posted inside the ground advertising the time of their next lecture. You simply watched them train and listened to them speak about the game and then went home without realising you had absorbed so much sound information until the next time

B

there was a game and suddenly realised you had done something right for a change. They were a coaching manual brought to life.

There was never any resentment, either, that around them were a group of young men who would one day be taking over their jobs and were, in fact, actively working towards the time when they could possibly have them before the older ones had finished with them. This bunch knew they were the best, who could prove it on demand if necessary, and approached life itself in the same extraordinary fashion.

Ronnie Simpson was, in football terms, already an elderly man when he joined Celtic in the first place and I always remember he accepted the good and bad that came his way with a facial expression that was the deadpan look of someone who had seen it all before. Jim Craig was the one I got to know best. Every day I was told to stand at a particular spot near my house in Drumchapel and he would pick me up by car for training. Ultimately I would replace him in the Celtic side but Jim, who was a dentist by profession, charged nothing for a daily consultation, during which he tried to pass on the benefits of an education at the highest level in the game.

There was a camaraderie amongst the European Cup-winning team that enabled them to get over the fact that some were studious, like Jim Craig and Billy McNeill, whose background had earlier been in accountancy, while others like Tommy Gemmell, Jimmy Johnstone, Willie Wallace, Bobby Lennox and Bobby Murdoch, were honours graduates from the school of life. The Lisbon Lions were not gifted choirboys but men who played hard, and occasionally lived hard, too.

There were others, like Steve Chalmers, the scorer of the winning goal in Lisbon, who were totally unassuming. Steve simply relaxed away from it all with a game of golf. John Clark had an encyclopaedic knowledge of football throughout Europe and in his typically quiet way seemed to attract a cluster of reserves around him to listen to what he had to say without anyone realising it was happening. It reminded me of the way his sweeper's role in the side went unnoticed until after he had done his work.

The Lions have been a legend for twenty years now and Scottish football suffered, perhaps, from the fact that the Celtic side of 1967 was so good domestically there was no-one at home able to then rise above themselves in European competition and help Jock Stein's side create a pedigree for this country at that level.

The mood of the club was to change, though, after Feyenoord

had beaten Celtic in extra time on the night the legend was dimmed in disturbing circumstances. It would be said afterwards that the Celtic squad had become obsessed with money and had allowed that to interfere with their approach to the game. The players had often spoken privately about what they considered to be the disappointing bonus paid to them after Lisbon, and the announcement of a commercial pool being set up, which was made the day after the final in Milan, gave their critics a day out. The truth of the matter was actually far nearer to home and even harder to take for a man like Jock Stein.

Celtic had, for once, underestimated the quality of the opposition. No-one had read the signs coming from Dutch football and foreseen that Milan would detonate an explosion at club and international level in that country. Watching from the stand with Kenny Dalglish, even we were not so naive we could see that when Celtic took the lead through Tommy Gemmell after half an hour it was not the same as putting a down payment on a win. Feyenoord equalised two minutes later and had in Wim Van Hanegem a player so underrated it was, for Celtic, like finding the house unexpectedly filled with woodworm.

This all led to a collapse in the time added on, with Ove Kindvall scoring the winner and the bitter realisation dawning that the better team had won. It was an irritating feeling that Jock Stein was not used to. His players had taken a European Cup final for granted and that was the signal for a change of direction to be taken so far as he was concerned. Sitting in the ground, trying to forget the game but never to erase the memory of what had taken place, the only reaction possible was to promise yourself you would never let it happen to a team you were a part of.

While the gradual break-up of the side was carried out, though, the basic machinery was not in any way faulty. The more experienced Celtic players could still carry an enthusiastic amateur like Danny McGrain, which was exactly how I regarded myself. If I had been asked then to sum up my capabilities, I would have said that I was a functional full back, no more, no less.

In the 1970-71 season I played seven league games, knew the experience of taking part in four League Cup ties, including a semi final with replay, but not getting into the team for Hampden on the big day itself, and adding a couple of European Cup ties to those minor achievements against Kokkola of Finland. Since that first-round tie in September of 1970 finished up 14-0 on aggregate it was a typically cool introduction to the scheme of things at Celtic Park, especially the second leg. Played 150 miles from the Arctic Circle, this was the most northerly tie ever played in the competition. Not bad for starters. All around me, though, the transformation was taking place. Tommy Gemmell was transferred midway through the following season and, since I had not appeared for some months, this offered me renewed hope. It was a feeling justified in the most unexpected manner, though. The quarter finals of the European Cup are not the kind of place where you normally make your debut in any given season, but there was such a heavy build-up of traffic for the full-back positions at Celtic Park by then I didn't stop to ask big Jock if he meant me when I was pulled into the team for the game against Ujpest Dozsa in Budapest.

It was one of the most remarkable afternoons in Celtic's history, with a goal from Lou Macari winning the game for us by 2-1 in the last five minutes after we had earlier taken the lead through an own goal from Horvath that was later equalised by the same Hungarian player. When a man who had seen and done as much as Jock Stein could say afterwards that it was the finest-ever display by a Celtic side on that kind of stage, especially considering the average age of a team that had in it people like myself, Lou Macari, George Connolly and Kenny Dalglish, then you knew you had taken part in something special.

An injury to Jim Craig had given me my chance and I held on to my place until the return leg at Celtic Park two weeks later, which was watched by a crowd of 75,000. Even though Anton Dunai levelled the tie on aggregate only five minutes into that game, Lou Macari produced another vital goal for Celtic and we had made it into one more European Cup semi final. Celtic would be drawn against Inter Milan in the first meeting of the two sides since Lisbon five years earlier. It was a tie that gripped the imagination of the public in two countries, but there would be no part for Danny McGrain to play in either game. In fact, within a matter of days after the young Celtic side's breathtaking performance against Ujpest Dozsa, there would be a doubt about me ever playing football again.

March 25, 1972 is a date I will always have cause to remember. Celtic had gone to play Falkirk at Brockville while enjoying what had become our customary place at the top of the league, only awaiting official confirmation of our seventh championship in a row. The game was just six minutes old when I went for a clearance as it came out of the air, trying to instigate another Celtic attack. I distinctly remember glancing out the corner of my eye and seeing one of the

Falkirk players, Dougie Somner, coming in to challenge. And then the lights went out.

Recollection is hazy after that. Neil Mochan, Celtic's trainer, put smelling salts under my nose and I vaguely recall running up and down the track beside the touchline waiting for my head to clear. I must have felt better than I really was, or tried to show a willingness to soldier on for the team, because I came back on and actually played out the rest of the first half.

To be frank, Brockville is not every player's dream ground and as we sat in the dressing room during the interval Lou Macari, who was the substitute that day, more or less insisted that I do a pal a favour and go back on because he wasn't exactly thrilled at the prospect of taking my place. I tried my level best to oblige but as I stood up to go out the whole of Central Region seemed to turn at a 180° angle and I announced to no-one in particular that I felt very sick.

It was like being in a dream sequence after that with people's faces appearing, disappearing and then re-appearing saying things I didn't understand. When I heard the sound of the ambulance bells, I wondered who it had been called for and was only partly conscious when I was admitted to Falkirk Infirmary.

Laraine had not been at the match, even though we had been married just eight weeks before that at a church near her parents' home in the West End of Glasgow. The ceremony took place during the power cuts caused by a national dispute, and as we tried to sign the wedding register all the lights in the vestry went out, which shows you that for a football player all contractual negotiations are difficult, even the marriage contract!

I might have been back inside the church for all I knew about the two days after the match at Brockville. There was no operation or treatment of any kind, and so far as I am told there were not even any external signs of an accident having taken place, but the nurses and doctors could not let me sleep for forty-eight hours.

Every couple of hours they would come to look into my eyes and make sure they were not filling up with blood, the sign of internal bleeding from the brain. I had fractured my skull, and for some people it is probably what I am best known for, even those who would be hard pushed to tell you which team I played for. Head injuries of that type were not common then, which was probably just as well or I might have known to be far more worried than I ever was about the whole business.

All I felt as I lay in bed was an overwhelming urge to sleep. Sean

Fallon was considerate enough to bring Laraine to the hospital and I remember Billy McNeill's wife, Liz, arriving with one of their daughters to visit me, but I was coming and going to the extent that there was talk outside my door of moving me to a neuro-surgical hospital in Edinburgh. It was decided after another week that I could go home, though, on condition that I did nothing strenuous and attended Glasgow's Southern General Hospital. Probably to prove to myself as much as anyone else that there was no legacy from the accident, I got up one day and decided I would learn to drive a car. It may have taken me twenty lessons from a very patient tutor but I got my licence at the first attempt and the next time I went to work at Celtic Park I did so under my own steam in more ways than one.

First of all, though, I had to live with the suspicion that there might not be a career to resume. Every morning I opened my eyes and hoped that the double vision, which had been a permanent difficulty since the clash of heads, would go away, but for a month it never did. I had nothing to go on where a skull fracture was concerned, either. There was nobody to speak to in order to get advice or even moral support. All I knew was that I needed to restore my confidence and I began by sitting at home heading a child's balloon, working on the principle that every recovery has to start somewhere.

No one at the hospital had ever said anything to me about my future in all of the four months that I went there as an out patient, until the day, that is, I was told I was going for the test that would determine whether or not I could play football again. Just like that! I had been keeping calm and then, all of a sudden, I was being offered an even money bet on the rest of my professional life at the age of twenty-two. Electrodes were strapped on to my head, which was just as well under the circumstances. If I had been put on to a cardiograph instead, I think I would have been removed to the coronary unit at speed. The verdict, in any case, was that I had made a complete recovery.

Years later, by a remarkable and tragic coincidence, a similar, but not identical, injury would beset my cousin, also called Danny McGrain, who played for Clyde. Danny did not fracture his skull, as was commonly thought at the time. A ferocious shot stopped by his head burst a blood vessel at the back of his skull. A blow to that part of his head would have caused that to happen, anyway, so it had nothing to do with football as such. Had it not occurred during a game, however, Danny might not have been attended to straight away and could have bled to death. As it happened, he was raced into intensive care, and although Danny tried to make a comeback it was ruled as being medically inadvisable and he had to give up the game to which he could have offered so much. If anyone should feel grateful, then, that he was able to carry on and make a living from football, and with no side effects whatsoever from a fractured skull, it is the Danny McGrain who was luckier than that.

The road back was made even easier for me because of the patience and consideration shown to me by various people at Celtic Park. I suspect that Jock Stein ordered there to be no jokes at my expense in the dressing room until he had made up his own mind when my recuperation could become a laughing matter. Every day the normal, stamina-building training that would lead Celtic into the 1972-73 season ended with the manager taking me on my own for heading practice, beginning with a rubber ball and progressing to the stage where I would have no qualms about putting my head in the way of a cannonball.

That was how it felt when I finished with the theoretical work and passed the practical test that would make my skull fracture cease to be a topic of conversation. Bertie Miller of Aberdeen was not a particularly tall or muscular man but he could crack the ball with the best of them. When, early in the season, I got in the way of one of Bertie's shots with my head the impact was enough to send me reeling to the ground. I could sense the crowd momentarily hush and knew that Neil Mochan would be crouched at the mouth of the dug-out ready to race on and see if I needed help. The stars cleared and the bells stopped ringing, though, and I was finally back to being someone looking to make his way in the game.

The way was made wider for me to come through when Jim Craig decided to leave Celtic and play in South Africa for a year. It was a season of mixed blessings and also the one that made me feel I might not be such a bad player after all, having by then completed the five years at Celtic Park that would be considered a full apprenticeship in any other walk of life.

Playing in all but four of the club's league matches, I won my first championship medal on the very last day when Celtic defeated Hibs at Easter Road to take the title by one point from Rangers. Hibs, though, had also been the cause of one of my severe disappointments six months earlier when they beat Celtic in my first Cup final appearance at Hampden. If the championship seemed to be under Celtic's influence, the spell had a habit of failing to work at Hampden. Losing the 1973 Scottish Cup final there was an even bigger setback. It was the S.F.A.'s Centenary final and, fittingly, it was contested by Celtic and Rangers in front of almost 123,000 people. Our oldest rivals hadn't won the trophy for seven years but, like the sentence imposed after breaking a mirror, their bad luck had finally expired and although we took the lead, and even equalised after Rangers had then gone in front, it was not to be our day.

With an hour gone, the fifth and winning goal came when Tom Forsyth of Rangers, who looked like a tourist standing that far up the park, scored from the distance all players like best, which is roughly two inches from the goal-line. The fact that he still managed almost to miss it made matters even worse. The gaining of my first full cap for Scotland a week later meant I did not have too long to dwell on losing such a prestigious match. It was the late Willie Ormond who was in charge of the national side by then, and I would always side with those who said he was one of the wisest national managers we ever had, and not because he picked me! Willie gave me my first representative honour as a senior earlier that season against England at Rugby Park. It was the second cap that merited a place in my memoirs, though, when I played against Wales for the Under 23 side. It was there I first came up against a winger called Leighton James. We would become widely publicised duellists for many years after that, but it was just as well for Leighton there were never any pistols involved or he would very likely have shot himself in the foot. The man simply could not find a way past me and his sense of fair play went with his temper on numerous occasions. Gradually, like all opponents who are losing the place, he became a compulsive talker during the matches we had against each other. None of it was fit for consumption here: all of it followed the general, and tired, theme that I came from a country where nobody who played in the national jersey had parents who were married to each other.

We beat Wales at Under 23 and full international level that season, and although Northern Ireland and England then defeated Willie Ormond's team in the Home International Series there was a journey to Switzerland immediately afterwards to take the sting out of that. Not that there was much relief for the manager, unfortunately for him, because it was *en route* from Glasgow to Berne that one of my Celtic teammates, George Connolly, first performed one of his infamous disappearing acts. I will always remember the look on Willie Ormond's face as he was told what had happened when we assembled on arrival. There were so many players and officials, he simply hadn't noticed the biggest man in the party had gone missing, quietly making his exit via the toilets at Glasgow Airport.

Less than a month before, George Connolly had been named Scotland's Footballer of the Year, and deservedly so. He was a highly gifted, technically skilled and tremendously cool player. George, though, had a temperament that was as fragile as porcelain. To this day, I would not regard myself as a particularly outgoing person but, coming from the city of Glasgow, I have been born with a certain resilient streak in my character and blessed with a fair degree of good humour. Next to George I must have seemed like Bob Hope.

George Connolly came to Celtic Park from a small village in Fife and he never shook the country dust from under his feet. He was always uncomfortable in the public eye and would probably have been happier working as a long-distance lorry driver during the week with a Saturday off to play football. I worked on the principle that Glasgow was my hometown as much as the supporters' and that I would never let the thought of being recognised put me off going anywhere.

At Celtic Park in 1973 we had new players by then like Dixie Deans, who had the West of Scotland character role off to a tee, so it was as necessary to live on your wits in the dressing room as it was on the park. Dixie was a great loss to the stage, in fact, but one day big George failed to see the funny side of a joke aimed at him and without waiting for the first bell the two of them were rolling around on the floor exchanging blows. It took six of us to finally pull them apart.

George was the nearest thing Scotland had to the legendary Franz Beckenbauer of West Germany but he could not adapt to the big time and he was out of football altogether by the age of twenty-six. After the airport episode I knew instinctively his career was finished. The loss to the game was incalculable but the real losers, and the people I really felt sorry for, were George's family. I have never seen him since the last day he walked disconsolately out of Celtic Park.

It was, then, an eventful time. A friend had fallen by the wayside but my career had righted itself after a serious mishap. I was beginning to learn that this was how life could be in the game.

During the close season, Laraine and myself took the first car we had bought, a very modest and slightly beaten-up red Volkswagen, on a touring holiday of Scotland to slow down and take stock of all that had happened. The journey took us to John O' Groats, which seemed fair enough after feeling I had been at Land's End twelve months earlier. There was much to look forward to. With five full international caps to my name, the coming season offered the promise of playing in a World Cup tie for the first time and helping Scotland get to West Germany for the finals, something the country had never managed before.

A world record-equalling ninth league championship in succession stretched before Celtic on the domestic front. Both aims would ultimately be achieved, too, but for Danny McGrain there would, as usual, be a levy to be paid along the way.

4

Diabetes

If illness is Mother Nature's way of telling a person to slow down, I was in too much of a hurry to pay any attention either before, during or after the discovery of my diabetic condition in the Summer of 1974. Before that year had even come in there was the totally new experience of qualifying for the World Cup finals as part of the Scotland team, and then Hampden Park once again chose to deny the existence of the law of averages where my Cup Final appearances there were concerned.

To lose any match of the importance of a national final is bad enough, but when you have been looking for third time lucky and what you get is the lowest crowd of modern times for a game that kicked off at 1.30 p.m. in temperatures that were as low as the spectator's spirits, then it is even harder to take.

That was how it felt when Celtic went down to Dundee in the League Cup final staged at midday in December because of nationwide power cuts and lost when I slipped on the treacherous surface as Gordon Wallace turned and shot with only fifteen minutes left for play. The irony was that whenever I appeared on the same ground in a dark blue jersey very little seemed to go wrong. This was best illustrated the previous September when Scotland defeated Czechoslovakia to reach the World Cup finals for the first time. The atmosphere that night was exhilarating after Jim Holton had equalised an opening goal for the Czechs that might have demoralised lesser opposition but only inspired us. When Joe Jordan came on as a substitute and scored the winner, I am sure I listened to my own heartbeat from then until the final whistle.

The reaction of the Scotland players after that also showed how deliriously distracted we were in the moment that we had created a genuine milestone. I swopped my jersey with one of the other side, for instance, but I have no idea even now of who it was. I only wish I did or I would write to him and ask for it back. It was a priceless souvenir I let slip through my hands, but by then none of us were really responsible for our actions.

There was an overwhelming urge to celebrate as we had never done before, so Kenny Dalglish, Ally Hunter, who was then also

Celtic's goalkeeper, and myself decided we would take our wives to a casino in the centre of Glasgow for a drink. None of us actually being drinkers, though, we did not think about minute details like licensing hours. When we got there the bar was closed and there was no late extension, World Cup or no World Cup. The biggest night in the country's football history up until then, and three of the team recognised it by drinking milk. And that is the absolute truth.

It was a time to be completely frank about your habits in that direction, too, because thereafter Scotland's national squad would be involved in a sequence of controversial incidents that were drink-related and caused a bemused general public to believe that we were basically unruly and a disgrace to Willie Ormond, who had the misfortune to be in charge of us. The fact is that no-one ever let Willie down on the park because we all had too much affection for the man to do that, but certain individuals tried to get away with murder in what we shall call their social hours. The squad was not overrun with trainee alcoholics but there were some who could not handle one drink too many. As a rule footballers tend to believe they are above the law, whether it is the S.F.A.'s code of conduct or the rule of the land. This is clearly not the case and there were some spectacular examples to come of how that lesson would be learned the hard way.

In between times, however, Celtic moved confidently towards their ninth championship in a row, equalling the world record held by M.T.K. Budapest of Hungary and the Bulgarian side, C.D.N.A. Sofia. That achievement would have stood on its own without any difficulty but it was made all the more commendable because, along the way, we overcame disappointment like the League Cup final defeat and then the nonsense of the European Cup semi final tie with Atletico Madrid, which could have had a damaging effect on everyone at Celtic Park.

Only those who have since had hypno-therapy to blot out the memory could ever forget the first leg of that game in Glasgow. The Spaniards had three men, Quique, Ayala and Diaz, sent off and a total of seven booked in a match that ended without a goal, which was hardly surprising since play only took place in between interruptions for acts of violence. I had been made a substitute that night but as I moved towards the tunnel at the end I knew instinctively that the physical aspect of the evening would not abate with the final whistle. I did not have to wait too long to be proved correct, either. There took place what is still referred to at Celtic Park as the post-match cabaret, when our exemplary discipline over the ninety minutes gave way to a much-needed release of tension.

There is one Spanish player in particular who will no doubt remember how revenge was visited upon him by someone who is still at Celtic Park to this day. The party was broken up, out of sight of the crowd, by the Glasgow police. It was against this background, then, that Celtic travelled to Madrid, under protest, to play the second leg. By then it was obvious that Atletico had used players who were expendable in Glasgow in order to get a tight result. The real team would meet us in the Ramon Calderon Stadium.

Meanwhile, our supporters, who had already booked places on a charter flight, were advised not to travel and the British ambassador in Madrid, Sir John Russell, was invited to the match as a neutral observer. It was obviously not going to be a friendly, although when Jimmy Johnstone announced on arrival at our hotel that he had received a death threat by telephone to his room our first reaction was to dissolve with laughter.

In the end Atletico won comfortably and, having played in the game, I can appreciate now that they were a highly talented side.

If this made it all the more surprising that they should have resorted to so many underhand tricks at Celtic Park, I can only say that I was left wondering, and not for the first time, about the behaviour of the continentals. We will never be able to live with them for the variety of their repertoire when it comes to painful encounters off the ball, although there are times when I honestly wish we would give it a bit more thought, and yet they are marvellous players who could easily get by without creating mayhem.

Madrid was not allowed to prey on our minds, in any case, because Celtic returned to play Falkirk just three days later and got the draw that was enough to win us the title. Nine championships in a row will, in my estimation, never be won again by any side. The difference between then and now is that clubs like Aberdeen and Dundee United have emerged under the umbrella of the Premier Division and grown in stature to the extent that a monopoly on that scale would not be feasible. What I can foresee, though, is Rangers becoming the foremost club in Scotland for a very long time to come. Their power base lies in the phenomenal wealth of the club, which will enable them to continue buying first-rate professionals who are already the finished article and will help carry on Rangers' domination.

This will, in turn, keep the gates at an incredibly high level and so provide the club with the money to make sure the supply of championship stock does not dry up. It could be the Celtic supporters' definition of a vicious circle. The only club who can live with that kind of challenge are Celtic, though, but in order to match Rangers they will need to generate spending money, and be willing to use it, in a way that has so far been foreign to the directors' nature. I have views of my own on how this could be done, which I will outline later on.

In 1974, though, such a topic of conversation could not have arisen because Celtic were then the kind of team that had an aura around them the like of which could still terrify the opposing side, such as happened in the Scottish Cup final against Dundee United. Jim McLean had only been in charge at Tannadice for three years by then but had taken them to their first-ever final with a side that contained youngsters like Andy Gray, who was then only eighteen years old, and Graeme Payne. On the day they must have felt that the Hampden bowl was like being trapped inside a microwave oven that had been switched on.

Celtic were two goals up, through Harry Hood and Steve Murray, after only twenty-five minutes' play and the game was as good as over. I had started the match although, for once, I had kept it from Jock Stein that I was feeling less than one hundred per cent fit. The symptoms were not like anything I could have described to the manager, anyway. All I knew was that for an athlete of twenty-four to feel that way there had to be something very wrong. It all passed off unnoticed and Tommy Callaghan took my place in the second half before Dixie Deans added a third, and final, goal to make it look as if everything had gone to plan.

The way I felt was enough to make me withdraw from the Home International with Northern Ireland the following week, however. Still unaware of what was happening to me, I came back in for the win over Wales at Hampden that was to lead up to one of those stories about player misbehaviour that have grown into legend. It revolved around what one of the more imaginative of the Scotland squad diplomatically tried to explain away to the press as a pre-breakfast fishing trip designed to help the players relax. Not surprisingly, no-one swallowed that.

First of all, most of us had been out all night, never mind concerning ourselves with what time breakfast was served, and, secondly, it relaxed Jimmy Johnstone to the extent that he could have died as a result of it.

Although I was still a strict teetotaller, I went with a group of players, including Billy Bremner, Denis Law, David Hay and Jimmy Johnstone, to a hotel nearby the team's headquarters at Largs, where the owner had provided us with a private bar outwith regular hours. Somewhere between four and five in the morning, as we made our way back along the front, Jimmy thought it would be amusing to jump into a rowing boat and, being very relaxed indeed, had no reservations about being given a shove out to sea by his friends. He was still unperturbed when he became a small dot on the horizon a few minutes later. It was only then, with Jimmy singing the Rod Stewart song, 'Sailing', which had been adopted as a football tune, that David Hay saw the more serious side.

Just to embellish the farcical side of the story, though, he set off to rescue Jimmy in an even smaller boat, using bits of wood that had been floating on the surface of the water as oars. I just stood there, transfixed and with my eyes closed, hoping neither of them would decide to go overboard and swim for it.

Largs is a residential area, not used to that level of noise and commotion in the dead of night, but no-one was more startled than Scotland's trainer, Hugh Allan. He wakened the manager, and Willie Ormond alerted the coastguard. It was a subdued bunch of would-be revellers who waited at the water's edge until the seafarers were safely returned. Jimmy Johnstone was blue with cold and had to have Denis Law's sweater wrapped around him to ward off pneumonia, which might explain why his language turned a similar colour when we eventually got back to our hotel. The landlady, because it was a glorified boarding house totally unsuited to a football team, had to come downstairs in her dressing gown, complete with hair in curlers, to let us in. She scolded us for our antics as if we were misguided children, except that Jimmy was in no mood to be lectured and made that clear in an explicit kind of way.

As I recall, Jimmy was the last one down from his bed to attend the meeting Willie Ormond convened later that day to discuss discipline. When he finally joined us, with the manager staring straight through him, Jimmy's response was, 'You are drawing me some dirty looks, are you not?' I thought Willie was going to fall off his seat at that point.

If you are a member of any Scotland team that beats England anywhere at anytime, there is not a man, woman or child in the country who would regard you as anything other than a national hero, or so it seems. Jimmy's slate was wiped clean, and the rest of us were forgiven as well, a few days after that episode, therefore, when a 2-0 win over England at Hampden sent us on our way to the World Cup with the nation's blessing. We had hardly waved goodbye, though, before the habitual offenders quickly found several more inches of hot water to jump into.

After a warm-up match in Belgium which we had lost by the odd goal in three, the Scotland party travelled to Oslo for the last of our exercise games on an aeroplane that soon became a skyborne saloon. It is not in any player's nature to find a way of saying no when he is being offered a lot of drink to be consumed on the premises, so to speak, as well as a carry out, and all of it for nothing. The sound of glass bottles clinking together inside carrier bags as we left the airport in Oslo was the cue for a day's carousing that ended with Jimmy Johnstone and Billy Bremner being asked to leave the bar at the place where the team were staying. This was ten days before our first-ever World Cup match, and the reaction of certain S.F.A. councillors among the official party was that examples should be made of the people involved, and that they should be sent home.

Apart from the fact that it would have been potentially fatal for morale to have the team captain and one of our most feared players made scapegoats like that, it would also have been a hypocritical decision.

Late-night revelry was not confined to the players. In the room next to mine at our World Cup camp in Frankfurt there would be two of the S.F.A.'s hierarchy who shared the liking for a party atmosphere. Not that I should complain because they actually helped, in an indirect way, to alert me to my diabetes.

One night, after I had been awakened by the noise, I found myself drinking orange juice by the pint and going to the bathroom every couple of hours. Our headquarters were not the most luxuriously appointed, and the room I shared with Willie Donnachie, then of Manchester City, had no bathroom, so I had to pass the festivities on a long walk to the communal toilet. It was getting to the stage where I was also asking Willie to carry up two pints of juice for me along with the two I had for myself before we went to bed at night. This was not taking into consideration the endless amounts of minerals I was taking during the day or the half-time breaks we had during the games against Zaire, Brazil and Yugoslavia in which I spent the whole time consuming fluids.

I was then suffering a dramatic weight loss of two stones in all, but in my own mind I was still putting everything down to the humidity in the air and to an excess of nervous tension.

Scotland's World Cup in West Germany was our best entry to date for the book of heroic failure. We were the only team in the whole tournament not to lose a game, yet we were eliminated on goal difference. All of that encouraged me to think I had simply run myself to a standstill like every other Scottish player. I have been told since that my condition would have been diagnosed for me had we gone any further in the competition because I would then have lapsed into a diabetic coma as matters were coming to a head. As it turned out, it was Laraine who was so shocked by my physical appearance when she joined ten thousand supporters to welcome us home at Glasgow airport that she insisted on getting medical advice. That night she made an appointment for me to see our family doctor the following day. I couldn't go to his surgery, though, because I was too weak to get out of bed. After the doctor's house call it was arranged that I be admitted immediately to the Victoria Infirmary in Glasgow for tests.

The doctor wanted an ambulance to take me there. I called for a taxi because I did not want anyone outside my own family to know of the problem. For a person who feels queasy at the thought of an injection to be told he is a diabetic is an unnerving experience. Even before I wondered about the consequences of this illness where my playing career was concerned, the idea of inoculating myself was causing me distress. Like everybody in that position, I was given an orange to practise on first of all and then told to pick my spot for the first go at the real thing. A leg is usually the favourite, but with my weight having fallen to just over nine stones I could find no superfluous flesh hanging on me there in which to inject the insulin. There is another part of the anatomy, though, which is always good for spare fat, and once I had learned to give a whole new meaning to the phrase 'bottoms up' I was out of hospital and rapidly recovering.

There are numerous reasons why a person can be a diabetic. The doctors in hospital told me that even flying the Atlantic too often can be a cause, but since I had never done that there had to be another explanation in my case. A severe bump on the head is another way and for a long time it was generally assumed that, having fractured my skull two years before, the puzzle had been solved. It was not that at all, though, because my own curiosity led me to discover that my mother's brother had been a diabetic, thereby making it a hereditary problem. Why it should have affected me and no-one else is a mystery but I am only too happy to say that it has not been passed on to any of my three daughters.

Being a diabetic has never caused me to miss a game of football in the last thirteen years, either, even when I have suffered a severe side-effect known as a hypo-glycaemia attack. This is the medical term for any imbalance in a diabetic's insulin intake which sparks off an uncomfortable reaction that first causes the sufferer to act as if he is drunk. The next stage is to fall into a deep sleep.

The first time it happened to me I was already in my own bed at home. I came to feeling a terrible pain in my arm, only to find a doctor hovering over me having just given me an injection. That was in the early hours of a Saturday morning and I was able to get up and play well a few hours later. I have never had an attack on the field but it did once happen to me watching Jim Watt in one of his title defences when he was the lightweight champion of the world.

Intense heat can bring on an attack and the heavy arc lights above the ring at the Kelvin Hall made me unwell. I made it home but then collapsed and had to be revived by a neighbour who was none too concerned about how he got a glucose drink down my throat. What really worried me on that occasion was that I was wearing a brand new, candy-coloured suit to the fight and that ruined it.

More seriously, as a result of my condition I have probably become the patron saint of diabetics in the eyes of some people. Being in the public eye I get letters, even thirteen years on, asking for advice. They are mainly from the parents of children who feel better able to handle their fear of diabetes because the one who plays football has it, too. I never advise on treatment, though, because that is a doctor's job, but I do attend discussion groups affiliated to the British Diabetic Association and speak at various forums if I think I can be of some use. There is no cure for diabetes but it is controllable and I can honestly say that I have felt fitter since 1974 than I did before that year.

Before I could admit that to myself, though, I wanted to prove that I had overcome the diabetes problem. I did not want people at the club thinking of me as a person with an illness first, a player second, or for anyone to feel sorry for me. For a long time only Jock Stein knew I was a diabetic, and by the time I returned to him after the World Cup, the hospital and the injections I had done enough road work on my own to convince myself I had the stamina to pick up my career as if nothing had ever happened.

It was a time when everybody at Celtic Park needed their full quota

of health and strength. David Hay had gone from the club in a
transfer to Chelsea during the close season and he was the kind of
determined person on the park that any side can ill afford to lose.
The World Cup finals had been his stage and when David went away
from Celtic Park the defence there was never quite the same again.
Strangely enough, the dead hand that had held us down in the
League Cup final was lifted from our shoulders at the outset of the
new season and we won the competition for the first time in four
years in a climax that would be long remembered, especially by Joe
Harper of Hibs, who scored a hat-trick at Hampden and still finished
up on the losing side.

Jimmy Johnstone was approaching the stage where he had given
all there was to give to Celtic. Not getting a game at all during the
World Cup finals, and the realisation that an otherwise illustrious
playing career would end with that distinction missing from his
record of achievements, was a heavy load for such a small figure to
carry around. His love of Celtic, and his well-known ability to resist
everything except temptation, coaxed him to play it from the heart
on what would turn out to be his last appearance for the club at
Hampden.

As if he was nostalgic for the past, Jimmy scored the first goal and
then went through the old routines without missing a trick, helping
us to turn a narrow interval lead of 2-1 into a second-half jamboree
that saw Dixie Deans complete a memorable hat-trick and Paul
Wilson and Steve Murray complete Celtic's reunion with how they
could play if they were in the mood.

The back half of the season, with the exception of the Scottish
Cup, would be calamitous. Only one defeat in nineteen league
matches had been suffered until we met Rangers at Ibrox in the
traditional New Year fixture, but a heavy loss there led to a collapse.
Just four of the remaining fifteen matches were won and the
championship was removed from Celtic Park where it had taken root
since 1966.

It was a time of change. The perfection of a gloriously sunny Cup
final afternoon was eclipsed by Billy McNeill's decision to retire after
the 3-1 defeat of Airdrie. Both Billy and Jock Stein had symbolised
Celtic's rebirth as a club from the moment, ten years earlier, when he
had headed the winning goal that had won them their first major
trophy in eight years, and only weeks after the manager had returned
to Celtic Park in that role.

If Lisbon in 1967 had truthfully been their finest hour together,

Celtic's worst performance in Europe since then would cloud Billy's last season as the team went out to Olympiakos of Greece in the first round.

Only Jock Stein's decision to stay with us at Celtic Park and not take over from Willie Ormond as manager of Scotland made the summer more tolerable as Jimmy Johnstone, another of the club's legendary figures, made his exit for the United States and the San Jose Earthquakes.

The old order was changing but at least the ultimate authority at Celtic Park would be there to navigate the club through the period of transition, or so we thought. The coming years would prove that it is comparatively easy to live with success, but that the authentic mark of character is how the competitor handles a series of setbacks. For the players at Celtic Park, these began with the most telling blow of all.

5

Transfers and Transition

Jock Stein was taken from Celtic on July 5, 1975 when his Mercedes was involved in a head-on collision with a Peugeot travelling on the wrong side of the dual carriageway on the A74 near Dumfries. It was early on a Sunday morning and I remember devouring every updated news bulletin on his condition as the big man started his long haul back from the brink of death. It never occurred to me then that the patient at Celtic Park would go into decline so quickly without the manager being there, but there were a number of things to the detriment of the club that went wrong in the full season he took off to recover from his horrific accident.

There was a phrase that Jock used to describe the psychological trauma of what happened to him as he returned from his holiday in Minorca that stuck in my mind because of its coincidental relevance to what was happening at his beloved club. 'You don't see all the damage,' Jock said, and that was true of the Celtic support, even though watching the team go through the entire season without a trophy and seeing it fail to beat Rangers once in five tries at the same time as going out of the Scottish Cup in the first round might have made them feel they had seen quite enough to be going on with.

None of this, I should stress straight away, ought to be construed as criticism of Sean Fallon in any way. When he was suddenly catapulted from being the assistant manager to the man in charge of Celtic, Sean did not get the moral support and practical backing of the players he was entitled to expect, and that went for the senior professionals who should have known better.

Celtic were Sean Fallon's life, which was more than could have been said for some of the people who let him down. Not unnaturally, though, he found it difficult to be shoved up to the front after ten years as the man behind Jock Stein. Sean may not have been the greatest tactician who ever lived but Jock Stein would have been a hard act for anyone to follow and the lack of respect shown him in his hour of need did not help matters.

The team went away to the Republic of Ireland to prepare for what was obviously going to be a trying season with no Jock Stein and no Billy McNeill at Celtic Park. The tone was set, though, when an experienced player, who had cost Celtic money, broke the curfew Sean had imposed at our hotel in Ballybofey and went out for a good drink. That made me particularly angry because it was another sign of people failing to appreciate how much hard work Sean did for Celtic and to what extent he lifted pressure from Jock Stein's shoulders.

The job of telling a youngster he was getting a free transfer from Celtic, for example, was never carried out by the manager: it was Sean who had to break the bad news. And as someone who had a younger brother who was released by Celtic, I know what a distressing business that can be. Jock Stein certainly needed Sean more than was ever apparent to the general public and Sean was also the man responsible for bringing so many young players to Celtic Park who went on to help the club win major trophies, myself and Kenny Dalglish to name but two.

Among the crop he inherited while the manager was in hospital, though, were enough passengers to fill a jumbo jet. Certainly, there were enough to make sure we never got off the ground that season. It was the first year of the newly constructed Premier League, too. As a player at the time, I had welcomed its introduction because it encouraged people to think more about the game. With every club meeting each other at the very least four times a season, it meant managers had to devise new ways of overcoming the opposition as if it were a game of chess. Out of it came two of the best managers Scotland has ever produced in Alex Ferguson and Jim McLean.

Their teams at Aberdeen and Dundee United were the products of the Premier League and that is the highest form of compliment that can be paid to the top ten formula. I would have paid my money at the gate to watch them play if I had not been too busy trying to stop them, and that is also the greatest tribute any footballer can pay his fellow professionals.

The Premier League was not, is not, absolutely perfect but it was better than the slow death the game in Scotland was undergoing in the early seventies. Gates everywhere had been dropping alarmingly and the reasons were transparently obvious. Celtic supporters, maybe even sated by our undiluted success in the decade before, were picking and choosing which games to watch and that meant that in an eighteen-team league, as it was prior to reconstruction, they were ignoring a lot of meaningless fixtures. Rangers, on the other hand, had not won a First Division championship for twelve years and there was therefore an understandable reduction in their attendance figures on a gradual basis.

Rangers supporters lost to Ibrox and the cause are people who are lost to the game altogether because they would never dream of watching anyone else. Any change in the game's structure should always be dictated by what the paying public want. And what they craved, even at Celtic Park and Ibrox, was a more intense form of competition. It has been with us now for eleven years and I would say the Premier League has definitely achieved what it set out to do, even if I might also have one or two personal reservations over the side effects it has caused.

A league with a small elite band of teams has created an atmosphere in which the result has become the most important thing of all and not the quality of performance. It has also heralded the end, by and large, of skilful players forming the majority at any given club and it has encouraged managers to blood ever more youngsters on a level that could not have been imagined when I first came under Jock Stein's guidance at Celtic Park only eight years before the inception of the Premier League.

The reason for the age restriction having gone by the board may have had something to do with the Premier League very quickly turning into a test of stamina and strength with very little time to think on the ball. It has undoubtedly stimulated interest once again, though, and that means any critical assessment has to be tempered by the thought that the game is a hit at the box office, which is all the justification the architects of the league need.

In the future, the public may decide it wants even more innovations, and the game's administration had better be prepared to look lively and give the customer what he, or she, wants, be it the penalty shoot-out, a kick-in instead of a throw-in or, hopefully, Summer football. I honestly believe if a referendum were to be held on the subject the Scottish fan would go for altering the timing of the season. I am also convinced it would have a beneficial effect on our displays at club level, and in Europe, and be of significant assistance to the national side.

Those who are against the idea raise arguments like supporters' holiday arrangements. Well, not everyone goes on holiday. They also say the heat could be too much for our players and that, if they were forced to try, it would change the way we traditionally play the game in this country. First of all I would like to know when it last got that warm in Scotland and then say, more seriously, that the heat does not seem to do the continentals much harm, and it is their style of play we need to learn from.

That is because they play on better, truer surfaces than we do and are therefore able to train morning and afternoon on polishing up their basic skills. How can we hope to do that (even on a Saturday) when playing on a frozen, rutted pitch at Cappielow on a bitterly cold day in January? It is actually counter-productive, in my opinion, to play in the dead of Winter just because that was how the founding fathers saw the game. When professional football started out in Scotland they had not foreseen the day when we would be playing against our fellow Europeans and steadily losing our self-esteem in that sphere because we couldn't make the transition from our basic brand of football to their more sophisticated version. And how can we ever do that if our teams are expected to go from playing on snow on a Saturday to a sun-kissed pitch abroad on the following Wednesday?

The players would vote for Summer football because, not unexpectedly, they like performing with the sun on their backs and I'm sure the fans would prefer to go to a match in their shirt sleeves rather than swathed in thermal wear to ward off the danger of hypothermia. Who does it suit, too, to have people hanging around for a news flash as late as a couple of hours before kick-off in order to find out if a pitch has passed an inspection, meaning a game can go ahead? Even if a pitch has undersoil heating, that is fine for the players who won't be asked to risk life and limb, but what about the spectators? How do they keep warm? The fundamental issue here, however, is that playing the game on a treacherous surface during the Winter is of assistance to only one type, and that is the performer who is not over-endowed with skill.

In 1975, Celtic had a mixture of the skilful, the inexperienced and some others who let down a faithful following that deserved better. Too many individuals inside the club did not care enough for the jersey that Jock Stein always said was for big, important men and would not shrink to accommodate lesser talents. He was totally correct. It could have been even worse, too, because before the new season got underway Kenny Dalglish asked for a transfer. It was such an unthinkable move that Celtic prepared a new, and acceptable, contract for him to sign within a fortnight and gave him the captaincy of the club as well in succession to Billy McNeill.

In twenty years with Celtic I never once asked for a transfer, was never approached, legally or otherwise, by any other club and was never threatened with a shift from Celtic Park, either. If I had been keeping a secret deal from Celtic and the public all these years, I could finally divulge the details here but I suspect that any prospects of another team being interested in me were shattered on the basis that I was a diabetic with a fractured skull by the time I was twenty-four years of age. With a medical case history like that, it doesn't matter how good a player you think you are!

The fractured skull having come just as I made my breakthrough into the first team at Celtic Park, any potential buyers would have put a stroke through my name there and then. And for all that I felt I had a good World Cup in West Germany in 1974, which could have given some managers outside Scotland second thoughts, my diabetic condition being diagnosed straight after our return was the last straw. The news of that was kept quiet for fully four years but there are no secrets inside the game. While we are on the subject, though, I can explode one particular myth about the transfer market and its dealings.

It is always imagined that whenever the Scotland team gathers the home-based players return to their clubs unsettled because they have spent days having their imaginations fired by tales of how much money they could be earning in the South. Perhaps I was unique in this respect but not one soul ever spoke to me on that subject, or hinted that their manager had put them up to sounding me out over a move from Celtic. Full backs, even internationalists, are not the most glamorous or sought-after individuals. If there is any private wheeling and dealing it must be done among the forwards, the more spectacular end of the business.

I can't say I have ever lost any sleep over the fact that I never played in England. Essentially I am the type happiest when closest to home but there were plenty of professional reasons why I never wanted to leave. For one thing I enjoyed being with a successful club winning medals and bonuses. For the life of me, I couldn't see anything wrong with that. Who knows how I might have reacted to going somewhere that meant a good living was harder to come by, or the effect that could have had on my game. English referees, too, might not have gone for my style of play and that could have led to the kind of trouble a person can live without. Plenty of people over the years have told me that I could have handled the change and since I stopped playing I have, I admit, had the odd twinge of regret, but not to the stage where I regard twenty years at Celtic Park as a major mistake in my life.

As I said, though, love of the club would become a divisive

problem in the dressing room as we came to terms with not having it all our own way for a change. There were signs that some players were going over the hill, and new arrivals like Peter Latchford, Johannes Edvaldsson, Ronnie Glavin and Johnny Doyle were taking time to settle down at Celtic Park.

For all that, we finished second in the league table and could have looked back at only one win in our last seven matches and wondered what might have been as we just failed to win the championship. The bottom line, however, was that Rangers finished first, so we might as well have been in twenty-second place. The club also reached its twelfth, successive League Cup final, but that competition had fallen out with us once again and Rangers waited round the corner to take that from us, too. The game that really illustrated what we were going through, however, was the Scottish Cup tie at Motherwell, which left us with Celtic's poorest showing in that tournament since I joined them in 1967.

Kenny Dalglish and Andy Lynch had actually given us a two-goal lead at Fir Park before the half-time interval. In front of 25,000 people, most of whom had been hoping the cup would save Celtic from bankruptcy in the honours department, we came out and lost three goals in the space of eighteen minutes. This was an indication of which way the wind was blowing and within six weeks we had committed another act of folly in the European Cup Winners Cup against a mediocre Eastern Bloc side called Sachsenring Zwickau.

In spite of having all the pressure, we could score only once (Kenny Dalglish), missed a penalty kick (Bobby Lennox) and then suffered the final indignity when the dreaded away goal was conceded two minutes from the end. Apart from all that, the evening went very well! The same East German player who scored at Celtic Park, with the name that was a gift from God to the headline writers, Blank, got the aggregate winner in the return game and thereafter the close season could not come quickly enough.

The blunt truth was that Celtic did not have enough good players out on the park but, as is usually the way, it was the person at the helm, in this case Sean Fallon, who got the blame. During the Summer he was stripped of his title of assistant manager, to be replaced by Davie McParland, and given the post of Youth Development Officer. Not much of a way, I remember thinking at the time, for Sean to celebrate his silver jubilee at Celtic Park. The poor efforts of some players with the club contributed towards Sean being demoted, and for that I used to wonder how those individuals concerned could get to sleep at night.

In a time of transition Celtic also dispensed with Ally Hunter, Harry Hood and Dixie Deans. After less than ten years at Celtic Park, Kenny Dalglish and myself had, in our mid-twenties, become the elder statesmen of the side. Substantial change was at hand, though, because Jock Stein felt well enough to return and there were a couple of remarkable signings made as well. The first of those was Pat Stanton from Hibs, and it was a great pity that he did not arrive at Celtic years before, and that he also had the gross misfortune to have his career there cut tragically short because of injury.

In the frenzied atmosphere of the Premier League, Pat, if he had been given longer, would have been the perfect teacher for someone like Roy Aitken. Roy had just come into the first team then, straight from school in Ayrshire. With a side that was trying to get over a disastrous season, there was no-one with sufficient time or experience to instruct someone so young. For a short time, however, Pat brought composure and thought to the place and it was put to immediate good use. I have always felt sorry for Roy, though, because he was thrown in at the deep end and has had to learn by his own mistakes ever since. For all that, he has become captain of Celtic and Scotland and is still an underrated talent. If enticing Pat Stanton from Easter Road, where he had been an institution for so many years, was an almost miraculous move by Jock Stein, his next ploy showed that he could still have given Rommel lessons on how to be a fox under pressure. Signing Alfie Conn from Spurs was masterly because, being formerly such an idol at Ibrox, the transfer seemed to take the breath away from everyone connected with Rangers.

They were sufficiently winded to let us win the league flag by nine points from them and their breathing was still irregular when Celtic won the Scottish Cup final, too. If losing only four matches all season in the league proved that our luck had undergone a remarkable transformation, Hampden on final day was another outstanding example of how the breaks even themselves out. The game was decided on a penalty given for hand-ball by Derek Johnstone of Rangers. Our taker, Andy Lynch, had only tried two penalty kicks in his entire career, both of them with his former club, Hearts, and had missed each time.

If Jock Stein's manner had changed after his lengthy convalescence, making him more mellow, the league and cup double proved that the tactical faculties were in the same old

working order. The effect on me was so great that I was named
Footballer of the Year at the end of that season. Partly because of my
displays for Scotland at that time as well, there were some who said
that I was generally considered to be the best right back in the world.
What does that mean, though? The term is too sweeping to be valid.
How could anyone have known there was not a better player in my
position going about in some far-flung corner of the world?

Any notions I might have had of believing that kind of exaggerated
praise were knocked out of my head by Scotland's visit to South
America in the close season prior to our qualification for the World
Cup finals on that continent the following year. It was an educational
experience. I learned from our opening game that Argentine
footballers are basically cheats. My first physical contact with one of
their side ended with this player writhing in agony at my feet and me
wearing that innocent expression that all professionals learn to
perfect. The only difference was that mine was absolutely genuine on
this occasion. As the referee came towards me I hoped he wouldn't
take my name for one reason alone. When a player gets cautioned,
he likes to think it has been for something worthwhile, like sorting
out a nuisance. I had no sense of satisfaction like that. As it turned
out, I wasn't booked then but I made up for that later in the match
and, yes, I did feel a contented glow about the tackle that got me into
bother.

Playing against Brazil in the world-famous Maracana Stadium,
which was our next stop-over, was a different type of lesson. I am not
the type to stand open-mouthed in awe, no matter the surroundings
or the opposition, which was just as well that night. My man to mark
was Paolo Caesar, who went past me the first couple of times in the
match as if I had never boarded the plane in Glasgow. To get over
the halfway line was, by the second half, a major achievement for
Scotland and by the end I could genuinely appreciate what people
meant when they said the Brazilians seemed able to dance over the
top of the grass.

If that is the kind of night that makes you a better player, I came
home from Rio de Janeiro much improved and ready to go out and
do some missionary work of my own as part of the Celtic side who
would tour Singapore and Australia before the start of the 1976-77
season. It was while in South America I had grown a beard for the
first time, and before Jock Stein had seen it he named me as the
new captain of the club.

Kenny Dalglish was just reaching the stage where he wanted to get away from Scotland and make a fresh start somewhere else. At the eleventh hour he decided there was no point, under the circumstances, in accompanying the team to the other side of the world. The manager telephoned me at home and explained the position. I was honoured to take over but I would rather have done so with a stronger feeling of elation. The loss of Kenny Dalglish was, I knew in my heart, a catastrophic blow. If I was confused, so was Jock Stein, though, when he met me at the airport before take-off and discovered the whiskers.

So far as the big man was concerned, footballers did not have facial hair, especially Celtic players, and that was that. Since we were leaving the country, he would say nothing about it but I knew his tone would change when the plane was coming in to land on the return flight home, and I wasn't wrong. It would have been stupid to refuse to shave it off and therefore take a stand on such a minor issue. I had only grown the thing to see how it would look and, hopefully, to cover the generous expanse of chin. There was an unspoken agreement to say nothing to each other on the subject while we were away.

My first game as captain of Celtic was therefore in the exotic setting of Singapore, but the first time I was recognised abroad since assuming that responsibility was in Melbourne. After checking into our hotel there the players gathered in the foyer, whereupon we all heard a voice calling out to Fergie. It had been so long since I was called that, since my schooldays in Drumchapel, in fact, that I instinctively looked around for this chap Fergie along with everyone else. Only my mother called me Fergus after I left school, but my middle name was a secret no longer when the person doing all the shouting turned out to be a former classmate of mine who had emigrated Down Under years before and who welcomed me like a long-lost brother.

The tour should have been good for reasons like that, players joking at each other's expense, forming a bond after staying and playing in each other's company for so long, but the good of it would never materialise because final confirmation on our return of Kenny Dalglish being sold to Liverpool badly affected the club and created a knock-on effect that took a long time to get over.

His transfer to England was not only a sorry day for Celtic but for the whole of Scottish football as well. Kenny was such a talent that he was the foremost personality in the country. Dalglish was worth the neutral going to pay his money at the turnstile. Because we had played together in Celtic sides from the age of seventeen onwards, Kenny and myself had developed a telepathic understanding. He was capable of making even a bad pass to him look like a good one and he has never in ten years been adequately replaced by Celtic. There was one young man who, had he stayed at Celtic Park, might have gone on to be another Dalglish, but I'll go into his career when we get to it. All I can say about Kenny Dalglish is that Celtic's loss was definitely Liverpool's gain. I know he felt his timing was just right, moving to Anfield as Kevin Keegan left there for German football, but, for me, Kenny is four times the player Kevin ever was, and I have played against both of them.

In 1977, at the outset of my tenth year with Celtic, there ought to have been a determination, though, to rise above Dalglish's departure. I was the captain and the others were members of a team who were the defending league champions and the holders of the Scottish Cup. I was saddened by the loss of my best friend but heartened by the thought of qualifying for a second, consecutive World Cup, this time in Argentina. At the age of twenty-seven, I was also supposed to be at the very peak of my capabilities and was being spoken of as one of the reasons why Scotland would make an even greater impact in that competition than they had done in West Germany four years earlier.

It was as if Kenny Dalglish had possessed second sight, though, and got out before the walls caved in on us. There was a private disaster waiting in the wings for me and a collective fall from grace at Celtic Park that brought consequences on a scale undreamt of. My life was about to take another turn for the worse to start it all off.

6

Taking the Cure

It is one of the enduring myths about the game of football in Scotland that there still exists a species who will gladly play for the jersey, to employ the expression commonly used to suggest that the person concerned would happily turn out for nothing because it was an honour and a privilege to be associated with a particular club. Those who are connected with Celtic are thought to be so fanatically devoted to them, for instance, that they would be the first to play for the glory alone. This is probably because in the eyes of those who support them Celtic are not a football team but a way of life. The club's origins of being formed to feed the needy poor in the East End of Glasgow give Celtic a romantic background, and it often occurred to me during my time with them that the directors at Celtic Park felt the players should still be doing people a favour. The people in question being the directors themselves.

I would re-emphasise that, after twenty years with Celtic, I have an intense feeling for them and especially for the people on the terracing who are devoted to the team, but the board should remember that loyalty is a two-way street. They have to keep faith with players and fans alike. One way is by reinvesting the money they take into the club by buying new players to maintain, and improve, the quality of the team. The other is by properly rewarding those who are already on the staff and making sure they stay content with Celtic. The modern-day professional footballer is no different from any other working man. He is selling his labour and looking for the most competitive rate he can find for his skills.

That is not to say if the player happens to be with Celtic he is being offensive to the memory of the club's charitable founders by asking for increased terms every now and then. Also, the directors are only the present custodians of the club's heritage. Celtic really belongs to the people and they are entitled to think their interests, which lie in having the best team in the country, are being properly looked after.

This was not the case in 1977 at the start of our most disastrous season in post-war history. The transfer of Kenny Dalglish to Liverpool had given Celtic spending money to the value of

£440,000, but before that had even become a topic for discussion the first league game of the season inflicted permanent damage to an already ailing side. Pat Stanton was taken off against Dundee United in a game that finished without a goal and was never seen again in a competitive match, announcing his retirement a year later after accepting the hopelessness of his injury. It was a devastating loss to a side who expected to profit from Pat's kind of experience. The same afternoon, Alfie Conn had to be helped off as well and was never restored to Celtic as the same kind of player.

If Jock Stein had been left visibly dispirited by the departure of Kenny Dalglish, the manager was now beleaguered and in need of Liverpool's money being removed from the bank vault and brought out into the open air where it could be put to good use. The most frequently voiced criticism of Celtic's directorate, though, is their seeming reluctance to spend the money they make, which always prompts the average supporter to ask, not unreasonably, what is it they do with it, in that case?

This would have been a perfectly valid question as the first quarter of the season came and went with Celtic winning only two matches. The money in reserve was plentiful by anyone's standards at that time and Liverpool's contribution was only on top of twelve, high-earning years since the time of Jock Stein's arrival and the acquisition of regular major prizes, won in front of gates that were huge and profitable. Celtic, though, made no attempt to replace Dalglish in particular with a worthy addition to the side. He was irreplaceable in that there was nobody of similar playing stature in the country, but a significant signing ought to have been made for the good of a depleted team and a support who expected a proper response to Celtic's difficulties. Instead, the club embarked on a series of deals that brought some players to the ground on loan, others as free transfers or as part of arranged swops, and one or two who came for nominal fees that would verify you only get what you pay for in terms of quality.

The exception to this was Tom McAdam, who cost £60,000 when he was bought from Dundee United and gave Celtic ten years of valuable service, both in attack and defence. At that time I was the only Scotland internationalist left at Celtic Park and was just seven games into my new role as the captain of the club when my career was once again blighted by serious injury, a mishap bad enough to create the impression that Celtic were jinxed. It would eventually cost me fifteen months out of my playing life and once again cast doubt

Me and The Gaffer. Jock Stein offers his congratulations after my home debut for Celtic against Morton in September 1970.

A word of advice from my chauffeur, Jim Craig. One of the legendary Lisbon Lions, I took his place in the side when he left Celtic in 1972.

Brockville, March, 1972: and the moment I have fallen to the ground after the clash of heads with Doug Somner that left me with a fractured skull.

Not exactly an oil painting, but there was an excuse. This is me lining up to play against England at Hampden in May 1974. The following month I was told I was suffering from diabetes.

The Class of '62, Kingsridge Secondary School in Drumchapel. Spot the boy. That's me, third pupil from the right in the second row. They don't make ties like that any more!

Happier times in a Scotland Jersey. As a future captain of my country this is me in 1979 doing my national duty and telling this veteran player what his name is.

This sporting life! If it's for a good cause I'll turn my hand to anything . . .

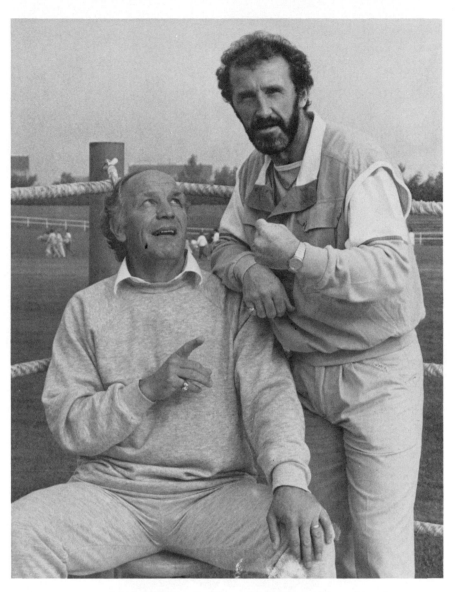

. . . and so will lots of others. He's a good boy, 'Arry!

Sometimes it is possible to get carried away, however.

In that case there was always one big man to watch over me and make sure he helped get the money to the people who help the less fortunate than ourselves.

Without hard work there is no reward at the end of the season.

All hail Caesar! Billy McNeill, as manager of Celtic, makes players work their legs off, as you can see.

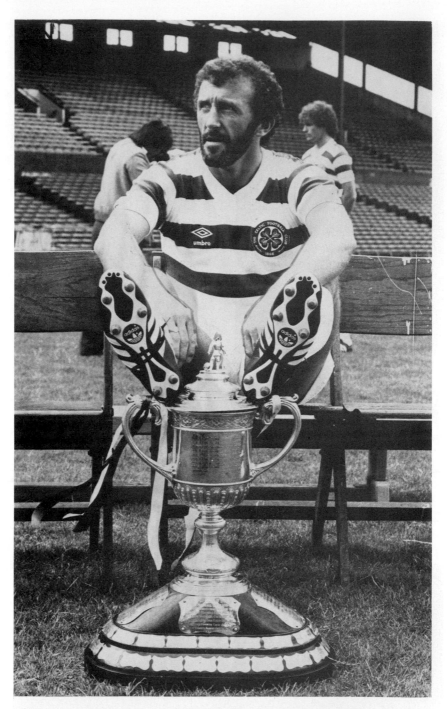

Some of us being older than the others had to put our feet up at the end of the season and the Scottish Cup makes a wonderful foot rest, if you can get your hands on it.

It was always worth it in the end, which is why we are all staring lovingly at the League Cup.

From my first Scottish Cup Winners Medal, here with the trophy won against Dundee United in 1974, this tournament held a special place in my affections.

The Scottish Cup can age a person, though. Myself and Hamish McAlpine before my last cup winners medal, also against Dundee United, in 1985.

over my career altogether, and yet the circumstances in which I hurt myself could not have been more innocuous.

John Blackley of Hibs was a close personal friend when we played against each other at Celtic Park on the first of October, 1977. I should make it clear he still is, as well. Because of that friendship I did not draw back, and neither did he, when we fought for a fifty-fifty ball on the edge of Hibs' penalty box. On reflection, I don't even know what I was doing that far up the park but I do remember only too well how much I felt every step of the way back up to the other end after our collision. The pain was quite something but, again because of our relationship, I tried not to show it since I did not want 'Sloop', as he is known to everybody, to see I had felt his challenge. When I finally looked back and saw he was lying on the ground receiving treatment I decided he had come off worst in any case. This was the all-time classic error of judgement.

Injured players were supposed to go into Celtic Park on a Sunday morning for an examination in those days, but I felt no reaction after the match and simply enjoyed the rest of my weekend. On the Monday morning, however, training was out of the question as a result of a shooting pain at the base of my foot. This was a full year before the coming of Brian Scott as physiotherapist to Celtic Park, and with him the electronic gadgetry that is essential to the treatment of sports-related injuries. I was told I had probably stood on a stone at the trackside during the match against Hibs and advised to put my foot into a bucket of ice!

By the following day the pain had shifted to another part of my foot and even a layman's diagnosis would have ruled out the stone theory. Whatever I had done, it was serious enough to force me to withdraw from that memorable night in Liverpool ten days later when Scotland beat Wales in a carnival atmosphere at Anfield and so qualified for the World Cup finals in Argentina. I consoled myself with the thought that, having already played in two internationals that season, Ally MacLeod, who was then Scotland's manager, would not forget about me and went off to have the obligatory x-rays done to locate the root of my trouble.

It became transparently obvious that all was not well when the x-rays proved inconclusive and I was sent with the minimum of public attention to a hospital in Manchester. The surgeon there had treated Jock Stein for the damage to his ankle done by the car accident a couple of years earlier and when I left to book myself into his care I was walking with a pronounced limp. Blood tests were carried out but no conclusions could be drawn from those, either, and I eventually left the hospital to stay with my colleague from the Scotland team, Willie Donnachie, to try remedial therapy under his trainer at Manchester City, Freddie Griffiths. Being an ex-rugby player, Freddie's methods had a heavy accent on the physical side, slogging up and down every terracing step at Maine Road and working myself into the ground at their gymnasium. It wouldn't be the first time I felt the back of Freddie's hand or the sole of his shoe as he encouraged me in his own way to forget that I was suffering from exhaustion.

It did all lead to a state of collapse one day, however, when I got the level of exercise and my intake of insulin mistakenly balanced and Freddie had to bring me round off the floor by pouring a glucose drink down my throat. That incident could have been enough to spread the word about my diabetes because it was made public knowledge in a Sunday newspaper, against my better judgement and wishes, soon afterwards. The fact that I was getting no better distracted me from taking too much notice of everyone now knowing something about me that I had been trying for years to keep quiet.

My case even came to the attention of a specialist in treating sportsmen at a clinic in the Welsh town of Oswestry and I was sent down there by Celtic to stay with him after he had written to the club. Dr Park, as he was called, tried a biopsy, which is the removal of skin tissue, and anything else he could think of, but the patient knew better than anyone there was no relief. Only Ally MacLeod had a go at easing the pain by the psychological ploy of naming me in Scotland's initial pool of forty players from which the World Cup squad would come. By then it had been six months since I kicked a ball in earnest.

I will never forget Ally for the kindness and consideration shown to me then, regularly checking on my progress and even offering to take me with the team to South America, presumably in the hope that I would heal up in a way that would be as mysterious as the complaint itself. To have accepted that invitation would have been wrong, though, and three weeks after the forty were named I reduced the number to thirty-nine by withdrawing myself from consideration. For all that, I never allowed myself to think my playing days were over and, in fairness to them, Celtic tried everything they could to support me in that belief. The late chairman of the club, Desmond White, in fact, was the one who offered to pay for Laraine and our daughters to accompany me on a six-week spell of treatment on the island of Minorca. Any possible cure was being given full consideration and it was thought the warm, salty waters of the Mediterranean might have healing powers. Unfortunately, all the holiday did for me was to send my weight ballooning up to fourteen stone from eleven stone, ten pounds. My depression increased, too, because it rained on every single day of those six weeks.

When I returned to Glasgow it was open season on how to cure Danny McGrain, including a spate of letters from Ireland. Some were from faith healers and others were from people suggesting old remedies that were a throwback to the days when superstition played a part in the treatment of illness. My personal favourite was the idea that I stand on a cow pat in the middle of a field of peat!

On a more practical level, Celtic sent me to another clinic instead. This one was for rheumatic sufferers and I was seen by a very impressively titled Professor Watson-Buchanan. Using a more sophisticated form of x-ray machinery which highlighted areas of inflammation, the precise spot causing me distress was isolated and I was told to come back in a month to have treatment prescribed. Having been in enough hospitals, and subjected to a sufficient number of examinations, to write a thesis on foot disorders for the British Medical Association, it was inevitable, I suppose, that I should eventually turn to alternative medicine at some stage.

Jimmy Steele has been acting as Celtic's masseur for thirty-eight of his seventy-three years and it was he who recommended me to visit Jan De Fries, an acupuncturist who works in the Ayrshire town of Largs. What gave me complete confidence in him straight away was that Jan offered me hope of renewing my career in the game. At our first private meeting, after his surgery had been cleared of all his other patients, Jan said he could tell what was wrong and gave me every indication that he would be able to clear up the problem as well. Can you imagine how reassuring it was to hear those words after more than a year of incapacity? After our first session there was a marked reduction in the foot's stiffness. A couple of days later it would go back to being immobile again, but after more acupuncture the feeling would gradually return to limbs that had not felt so supple in a long time.

I was encouraged enough to go back for my appointment with Professor Watson-Buchanan at the rheumatic clinic only out of courtesy, since I was anxious to tell him I had found the solution on my own. All I remember the professor saying, though, was that I stood in grave danger of losing my foot if I continued to play football. In his learned opinion I was finished, and he went on to ask me if I fancied going to a coaching job in Saudi Arabia, where he had contacts. The reasoning behind his medical opinion was just a muted sound in the background as I sat there in his consulting room reeling from the shock of it all.

I knew from personal experience of an acquaintance who had lost his leg completely that amputation was, in extreme cases, not uncommon among diabetics, but I had maintained all along that my foot problem had nothing at all to do with diabetes. For the first time in months I was walking freely and the leg that had grown thinner as a result of muscle wastage while it was encased in plaster was gaining in strength. I seemed too close to a recovery to settle for the last rites being read over my career. When the professor finished speaking I told him I was grateful for his trouble but that I was definitely going to make a comeback, and in the full expectation that there would be no tragic consequences, either. I then left his office even more determined a person than I had been when I walked in.

All the while the saga of my foot injury had been unfolding, it was also a necessary relief in a way from the events on the field involving Celtic. Jock Stein's last season as manager was one of unqualified misery, and on a scale that ought not to have been allowed by those who ran the club. The failing team, expiring for the want of fresh blood, lost fifteen matches in the Premier League and finished up in fifth place, which was not even good enough to qualify for Europe. The Scottish Cup ended ignominiously at the fourth-round stage when Celtic were knocked out, after first drawing at home, on the ground of a First Division side, Kilmarnock. The League Cup went into extra time and then into Rangers' possession, and the European Cup fully demonstrated how ill-prepared the club were to live up to their own reputation on the continent.

The Austrian side, S.W.W. Innsbruck, mercilessly exposed the deficiencies that were there for all to see in our defence and scored an away goal in Glasgow before taking us apart in their own country on a night when Andy Lynch was sent off and the aggregate score of 4-2 read like an obituary. Those who were there say that was the night Jock Stein gave informal notice that his time as manager of the club was at an end. If Jock had not wanted to give up his post at Celtic Park I believe he would have taken a stand and made life awkward for the club's directors. He had an obstinate streak and that is what makes me think he knew in his heart of hearts that it was all over.

The big man was mentally and physically tired. As it turned out, that was not to be a lasting condition but acting, he believed, in the best interests of the club Jock stepped down to make way for the only man who could have taken his place, Billy McNeill. In his time at Celtic Park Jock had won the club twenty-five trophies, the Scottish Championship ten times, the Scottish Cup eight times and six League Cups. The European Cup in Lisbon was, of course, the crowning glory. His place in the history books was as certain as the fact that he would be revered until the day he died by every Celtic supporter.

Billy McNeill had already given Celtic almost twenty years of his life as a player and was so steeped in the club that every defeat for them was like a stake driven through his heart. There was also no doubt that he was arrogant, moody and entirely what Celtic needed at that particular time. If the side lost badly Billy was quite capable of not speaking to the individuals he blamed for a week. He had a cutting tongue that could wither a person with a single phrase, such as the player who reported an injury to Billy after a bad result only to be asked if he had hurt himself coming out of the bath. The responsibility of management did not rest easily on his shoulders, either. When I was fit to play again I remember studying him closely one afternoon and being taken aback at how pale he had gone immediately before a Scottish Cup tie against Berwick Rangers. His mouth had drained of saliva and it was as if the blood had gone from his face at the same time, too, for fear of disgrace befalling Celtic against that particular team as it had done Rangers in the same competition eleven years before.

It may all sound extreme behaviour to the uninvolved but Billy's approach is really the only way to be if a person wants to be successful in club management. If you try to be too nice to players they will let you down every time, so that means keeping a fair distance between yourself and the staff.

He was aware that a new manager was at Celtic Park because the place needed to be sorted out. His initial reaction on his first day on the job, then, was to ask the players what they were laughing at if he detected signs of hilarity and then to ask them what their names were. Everybody was called out to the centre of the pitch and he introduced himself. At the end of his remarks Billy, who had told the players he was to be called Boss and nothing else, asked me if I had anything to say as team captain. When I replied, 'No, Billy' out of force of habit I could have kicked myself, but that was the last time I forgot my place and the rest of the squad jumped to attention thereafter as well. The present-day team would do well to take heed now that Billy is back where he belongs.

I had a lot to be grateful for where Billy McNeill was concerned. Along with John Clark, his assistant, Billy took me to Strathclyde Park every day after normal training to help me lose weight that had to come off before I could make a sincere attempt at coming back into the first team. Diabetics cannot diet in the way that other people can, so the full twenty-eight pounds had to be shed in sweat and in reserve games with hardly anybody watching as I tried to rediscover my timing with the ball and judgement in the tackle.

The acupuncture had made my foot as good as new again but to this day I have no idea what caused the injury that defied medical opinion. All I can say is I have never felt so much as a twinge in the last ten years. I was finally restored to the first team in Portugal, the country that will forever be associated with fond memories for all those with Celtic at heart. It was in Estoril, in fact, where Celtic had stayed before the European Cup final against Inter Milan twelve years before, that I played in a team who won 4-0 against the local side in a friendly match.

Billy McNeill had taken us there to find match practice and proper training facilities in the midst of a terrible Winter at home that was to turn out to be Celtic's greatest ally in that it bought us valuable time in the championship that season. When the freeze-up came, Morton had just beaten us to pull themselves above Celtic in the Premier Division.

With exactly half the league programme gone, we were in sixth place. The difference this time would be that Billy McNeill would not accept the situation as it stood and insisted on making two transfers that turned a struggling side into champions once again. When Davie Provan was bought from Kilmarnock for £120,000 it was a record transaction between two Scottish clubs. Six weeks later a player who was not even as well known, Murdo MacLeod from Dumbarton, arrived for £100,000 and then fate took a hand. Snow and ice kept us all waiting for almost three months to resume the league fixtures, by which time our new players had been familiarised with how it is Celtic play the game.

Billy McNeill was a sound tactician but inside he knew it was his duty to allow Celtic to be as spontaneous and innovative on the park as they could reasonably be. That is how the club have always approached the game, that is how the support will always insist they play it. Whenever people accuse Celtic of naivety, particularly in the sphere of European competition, I always hear at the back of my mind the anguished cries from the 'Jungle' to get the ball moving in a forward direction. If they were asked to watch the patient build-up from the back that is the essence of the continental game, the fans in Scotland would eventually find something else to do with their time on a Saturday afternoon. Rangers are finding this out, too. Graeme Souness knows how he wants his team to play but he will need to re-educate the club's following as he goes along because they want some of that old-time fervour to get them going. Souness' grounding was in the English league, of course, and from the time I spent there as Manchester City's guest I know that it is possible to watch games down South that would get football stopped if it were up to the Scottish supporter.

Manchester City themselves tend to be like Celtic in their belief that the public are there to be entertained, but there are a number of other clubs who could swop jerseys at half-time inside the dressing rooms and the crowd would never know the difference because they all play in the same, boring way.

By the time Celtic resumed after the impromptu Winter shutdown, in any case, the average Englishman would have had his breath totally taken away by what was to follow. The concluding half of our season, eighteen games long, was condensed into just two months' playing time, during which I took part in every match and even scored two goals in three weeks to propel us towards a fixture that will probably be numbered among the most memorable in Celtic's history and is known like a coded message to those who were there as the 4-2 game.

On May 21, 1979, Celtic needed to beat Rangers at home in order to win the title in Billy McNeill's first season as manager. We were a goal down and a man short after 65 minutes' play when first Bobby Russell scored and then our own John Doyle was sent off. Within a minute of that happening Roy Aitken had equalised and eight minutes after that George McCluskey put us in front in what was by that stage the atmosphere of the madhouse. Alex MacDonald got another one back for Rangers within a couple of minutes and that was how the score stayed until five minutes before the end when it was starting to look as if our hopes would be dashed in the cruellest way imaginable. Colin Jackson, Rangers' centre half, then had the misfortune to accidentally head the ball over his own line to put Celtic back in front. A game like that could only have ended on an even more incredible note and Murdo MacLeod's fourth goal for Celtic was hit with such power from well outside the penalty area that it looked as if he had been conserving his energy all season for that one moment.

Pandemonium would be too tame a description of what went on after that. Apart from the obligatory lap of honour there was bedlam inside the dressing room and boardroom afterwards but in the midst of it all I must admit I did sit quietly on my own for as long as I could get peace and thought about how I had felt a year earlier when celebration, and even playing, was the furthest thing from my mind.

Jock Stein had gone and my future looked uncertain. But how could I have asked for anything more by way of a start under Billy McNeill? When I reflect on both these men now I am determined to be a manager who will combine lessons learned from each one of them. Billy is a ferocious competitor who demands that players care about the game as much as he does. He can remember when they really did play for the jersey but he has also proved that he is a worldly man who knows that jerseys will not be accepted as legal tender when you are trying to pay the mortgage.

Jock Stein simply made it his business to know everything that went on at his club. He was on first-name terms with everybody behind the scenes at Celtic Park and with the members of their families as well. I can still see him first thing in the morning, long before training had begun, prowling the terracing steps picking up litter or uprooting a weed that had sprouted up somewhere, a man alone with his thoughts and letting the ideas that would improve Celtic fight for space in that fertile imagination of his.

He taught Billy McNeill well and I would be mad not to follow his example, too. Under Billy McNeill, though, there would never be a dull moment, that was the first thing I found out.

7

The Old Firm and Other Greats

When Celtic play Rangers in any Old Firm derby match, regardless of what it is for, this is known as the greatest club game in the world. Whoever first coined that grossly exaggerated description, however, could not have had football in mind at the time. This fixture means one set of fans with hatred in their hearts bellowing obscenities at the opposite end of the ground to another group of supporters who despise them with the same ferocity. Stuck in the middle of the mutual loathing society are twenty-two men trying to play a match.

My view of these occasions was properly formed, and rigidly changed at the same time, by the Scottish Cup final of 1980, which led to angry outbursts in the House of Commons and even the introduction of government legislation. The sponsors of the competition withdrew their patronage, too, and the General Assembly of the Church of Scotland managed a few words on the subject of grotesque scenes that brought disgrace upon the game itself.

It was indicative of the changing face of the Scottish League at that time that both Celtic and Rangers approached Hampden on final day knowing that the Scottish Cup was the only chance of a trophy that season for either club. We had been upstaged in the championship by Aberdeen and done out of the League Cup by Dundee United, who thereafter went under a collective title of their own, the New Firm. The level of expectation felt by the Celtic and Rangers supporters, therefore, would only be matched by the depths of despair that would be suffered by the loser. Just how degrading the demonstration of disappointment turned out to be would surprise even case-hardened veterans of such occasions like myself.

A total of 210 people were arrested either inside or outside Hampden amid scenes of rioting that caused policemen and women on horseback to draw their batons in Glasgow for the first time since the General Strike of 1926. Fifty policemen were injured as well as they tried to break up a battle on the pitch that had minutes before been the scene of great jubilation in the Celtic camp.

Celtic had gone into the game with a depleted side because two central defenders, Tom McAdam and Roddie McDonald, were under

S.F.A. suspension and the natural replacement for one of them, Jim Casey, had injured himself just two days before the final. The entire side had played a perfect, tactical game, though, with Michael Conroy and Roy Aitken performing heroics at the back. What had been a relatively sporting match then went into extra time and when George McCluskey deflected a shot from me past Peter McCloy in Rangers' goal in the time added on it seemed like the perfect end to my first experience of captaining the side in a national final, and at the age of thirty, too.

From the winners' rostrum I could see little pockets of unrest among the crowd, however, and felt there was the potential in the air for an escalation of the violence. Obviously neither I nor any other member of the Celtic team could have predicted what was to follow, though, after we had taken a run towards our own supporters to show them the cup, the traditional climax to such an afternoon. It was not until later that same night on the national news programmes we realised the full extent of the fighting that had taken place at Hampden.

Being the Protestant captain of the so-called Catholic club, Celtic, I had always been conscious of the religious divide that existed in Glasgow and beyond, a social disorder which used football to express itself rather than the game being the root cause of the problem. Occasionally, when I had gone to Ibrox to watch a match that did not involve Celtic, I had allowed taunts like 'half Catholic' to run off my back as I moved through the crowds but I honestly did not think both sets of fans had the capacity for an outbreak on the savage scale that was witnessed that day.

The match itself had done nothing to incite even the lunatic faction that go to Celtic-Rangers games, and it is a fact that Old Firm players take their responsibilities seriously in respect of law and order at these games because of their sensitive nature. There is next to no personal animosity between the players off the field, either.

I would count various Rangers players of the past and present as personal friends of mine, people like Sandy Jardine and Derek Johnstone, and Ally Dawson of the current side. This is not to say there are not those individuals who are provocative on the park when they are exposed to the heady, Old Firm atmosphere. Hugh Burns of Rangers is one who has always struck me as being that way and Celtic's Peter Grant comes into that category, too. They are fans in jerseys and that can be an awkward combination.

The only recent example of ill-feeling I can recall, though, would have been the Skol Cup final of 1986 when Maurice Johnston was sent off and made the sign of the cross before he left the field. That could certainly have been termed an inflammatory gesture given the aggravated state of play at the time, with Celtic losing to a late penalty kick and coins being thrown on to the park. In the recriminations that followed the Celtic board of directors made it clear they did not want to see players blessing themselves on the field but, speaking as a non-Catholic, I did not find that altogether fair or necessary.

There are players at Celtic Park like Pat Bonner and Tommy Burns who are devout believers in their religion. If Pat thinks it can be of some help to him in attempting to save a penalty kick, for instance, or Tommy finds it comforting to make the sign of the cross before he takes a penalty kick then I, for one, do not find that upsetting so long as it is done unobtrusively as a private demonstration of faith. It is not a spectator sport and that is why I found the same ritual hypocritical and out of place coming from Maurice Johnston as he was being shown the red card by the referee. The night before the Skol Cup final the Celtic squad stayed at the club's traditional base before Hampden at Seamill on the Ayrshire coast. All of the Catholic players in the squad attended mass on the Saturday night so that they could rest properly on the morning of the match the following day. All except one, that is, and there are absolutely no prizes for guessing the identity of the odd man out.

As a rule, though, Celtic and Rangers players mind their manners and curb excessive behaviour when playing each other. That was the reason why there was a feeling of resentment at Celtic Park in 1980 when the Secretary of State for Scotland, George Younger, criticised the Celtic players in parliament for celebrating the winning of the cup. He said that had provoked the trouble, which hardly seemed just. The S.F.A. held their own inquiry and they did not take that view. In their report they said that the Celtic fans had 'invaded the track and goal areas for the purpose of cavorting around and generally celebrating with the Celtic players who had chosen to run to that end of the ground, on the final whistle, to demonstrate to their supporters their exuberance at victory. At that stage of events there was nothing violent in the exchanges between players and fans. Rather it was a spontaneous, if misguided, expression of joy.'

Having said that, the S.F.A. Executive Committee still fined Celtic and Rangers £20,000 each, but not before the General Assembly of the Church of Scotland expressed their view that Rangers' policy of not signing Catholic players hardly took the heat out of the situation in general terms. If there was any good to come out of the entire affair it was that the riot helped bring into being the Criminal Justice (Scotland) Act, banning the carrying of alcohol into football grounds. I don't think there was serious doubt in anybody's mind that drink played a large part in bad behaviour on the terracing and contributed towards a substantial decline in attendances in those days. With this form of prohibition and the Scottish Cup's sponsorship going from a brewing concern to the Scottish Health Education Group the image of the game was altered along with supporters' attitudes, and all for the better.

Nothing will ever tone down the intense rivalry between the two clubs, but when the Old Firm match is referred to as the greatest game in the world it is surely a comment on the electricity in the air, where a player can get a standing ovation for winning a throw-in, and not on the standard of play.

I have been to games between Liverpool and Everton, for example, and these are models of self-restraint compared to what goes on at Ibrox and Celtic Park. Let us just say there is too much at stake for that ever to be the case in the city of Glasgow. The introduction of so many Englishmen at Ibrox has added a new dimension to the Old Firm match in that they get caught up in the tension but still try to play a bit of football wherever possible. On the whole, though, as it was in the beginning, so shall it always be when green jersey meets blue. Even in reserve matches between Celtic and Rangers you could cut the air with a knife. In one of my earliest experiences of the phenomenon I came off the park at Ibrox with marks of someone's fingernails all the way down my back.

The player in question was actually on his way out the door at Ibrox, having had one disagreement too many with the Rangers management. His commitment to whatever jersey he was playing in was still ferocious just the same. His name was Alex Ferguson. Not that I am holding up Alex's behaviour that day as being exemplary, but it was indicative of how wholehearted his approach to the game was, no matter what. By the time he went to Aberdeen as manager, Alex was widely acknowledged as one of the great coaches with an unbridled enthusiasm that he also demanded of his players.

The accolade of greatness is bestowed on people in football too easily nowadays but Alex Ferguson was a genuinely deserving case. He turned what I thought was a fair, but unexceptional side, into the most successful team in the country during the first half of the eighties. While winning Aberdeen their first championship flag since 1947, he began to show us what could be achieved with hard work. At one stage Celtic were ten points ahead of Aberdeen in the league during that 1979-1980 season but his players made up all of that ground and rounded off the chase by beating us twice in Glasgow. The fact that they also eliminated Celtic from the League Cup by defeating us home and away that same season proved that Alex was obviously capable of transmitting his fanatical will to win across to his staff.

Before he was finished, Alex created a team that was good enough to emulate both sides of the Old Firm by winning a European trophy. Aberdeen's achievement in overcoming the legendary Real Madrid in Gothenburg to win the European Cup Winners Cup was, to my way of thinking, every bit as praiseworthy as Celtic's win over Inter Milan in Lisbon sixteen years earlier. Ferguson had within his team players like Gordon Strachan who were inspirational. Jim McLean was, luckily for him, similarly blessed at Dundee United with Paul Sturrock. For me, the definition of greatness in a player is one who sets himself a standard of performance and maintains that level over a long number of years. Sturrock and Dundee United made their mark in 1980 with the winning of the League Cup, the first major trophy ever to come to Tannadice. They had to beat Celtic along the way to do so, and at Celtic Park, and look where that one success has taken the club since then.

On Celtic's road to winning the Scottish Cup we came across one player who many would argue was a viable contender for the title of the greatest ever produced by the British Isles: George Best. He was a member of the Hibs side Celtic knocked out in the semi finals at Hampden. At that time, of course, George was making one of his frequent comeback appearances that were strewn throughout a controversial career that started to go off the rails long before it should have done. On the day we met at Hampden, I was struck by his exceptional talent straight away. The stamina in his legs had long since gone but no amount of booze could dull a razor-sharp mind. By the end of the game he was tearing at that famous mane of hair of his out of sheer frustration because there was nobody on his own side who was quick enough to read George's intentions at one end of the park while Celtic scored five times at the other. I thought to myself at the end of the ninety minutes that day that I would not have liked to play against George too often when he was at his peak.

Strictly speaking, that was anything but true, though. In fact, it annoyed me intensely to think that it had taken us until 1980 to play against each other for the first time, and that we would never do so again in a competitive match. George ought to have played at the highest level for club and country far longer than he did, and in the final analysis it would have to be said of him that he cheated himself out of added years in the game, and wasted a tremendous gift, by succumbing too easily to temptation off the field. Best, though, allowed himself to become the first of the media-built personalities and fell victim to that in the end. No-one before him had been subjected to the kind of pressures George had to live with, although he brought a lot of it on himself, and it may be true to say that those who followed on after him learned by his mistakes. Most of them, at any rate.

By the time he arrived in Scotland, though, George struck me as being a solitary figure. I met him only once after that cup tie at Hampden and that was at a testimonial dinner for one of his team-mates at Easter Road, Arthur Duncan. My abiding memory of that night was that very few people actually went up to George, introduced themselves and then spoke to him, even though he seemed to be the most affable of men. Instead, they stood nearby and gawped at him as if he was on display, which could not have been easy for any person to handle.

If performers like George Best, Gordon Strachan and Paul Sturrock were truly extraordinary, though, there was coming along at Celtic Park at that time a teenager who was the equal of any of them. Charlie Nicholas came from Maryhill, across the road from where I had played my junior football when he was the age for starting primary school. My life had turned full circle in that I was now the veteran on Celtic's staff who was giving the younger players a lift to the ground every morning, as Jim Craig had once done for me.

Charlie's house was on my way into town, so I got to know him better than anyone over a number of years. He was the identikit picture people have in their mind of the gallus Glaswegian and he brought cheek to Celtic as well. Not arrogance, but an air of irrepressible confidence that endeared him to the rest of the players and to a support who loved him to the point of idolatry. They knew Charlie in the sense that he had been one of them on the terracing at Celtic Park not too long before, and Charlie gave them what they had come to see.

He came into the side when we were in need of a lift after a defeat from Rangers at the start of the 1980-81 season and scored six goals in his first five league games. With the help of his influence, Celtic went on to win back the league title and with a record number of matches won, twenty-six out of the thirty-six played. At the time I would have no hesitation in saying that Charlie had the undoubted potential to be the new Kenny Dalglish for Celtic and Scotland. I expected to see him better Kenny's total of caps and break the goalscoring record for his country. To me, Charlie was the complete player. As well as being absolutely lethal inside the penalty box, he had the brain to create openings from the middle of the park or anywhere else.

That is why if I was ever asked to state a preference for Charlie or one of his contemporaries, Maurice Johnston, I would go for Nicholas every time. Maurice can only be effective when he has the ball at his feet and the goal in his sights. Even in training, though, Charlie could make a fool of his team-mates, who knew his style off by heart. His repertoire of tricks was endless and the fans felt assured that Celtic would be successful so long as Charlie was in the team, and it seemed for a while that playing in a hooped jersey was all that mattered to him as well.

As they say in Maryhill or Drumchapel, Charlie's head was full of nonsense. He was just a bundle of good nature having the time of his life. I remember taking him for his first driving lesson in my car, which did not turn out to be the best idea I had ever had. We went to the car park of a quiet golf course in Milngavie on the outskirts of Glasgow. It was all a big joke to Charlie, especially the bit where he reversed the car at speed in the general direction of an iron fence and I let out the yell of a man who knew he was letting this long-haired teenager play havoc with his no claims bonus.

Being an Old Firm player, and living in the centre of Glasgow, does not stay Utopia for ever, though. Charlie would soon become the centre of unwanted attraction and a ready prey for those who delight in trying to upset people in his position. There was the story of a player with a club from a lower division who came up to Charlie in the pub that is used by the Celtic players after a match on a Saturday night and started to question his ability, saying that he was not the player the press and the fans made him out to be. After a long lecture on how this young man could do anything Charlie could do, and probably better, Charlie produced a twenty pound note from his pocket, very slowly ripped it in two, and then asked the by now embarrassed man in search of an argument if he could do that. Once he had turned on his heels and stormed off in the other direction, Charlie was quick to scour the floor for his money and borrow sellotape from behind the bar, I should add.

Boys who are brought up in the working-class districts of Glasgow know the full value of their hard-earned cash, and Charlie was not the type given to flaunting the fact that he was a high earner. The story, though, was proof of the fact that Charlie was outgrowing Glasgow. His career there with Celtic was, admittedly, all too brief, lasting only 111 games and taking up less than three seasons in total. It had the effect of a tornado, however, and when Charlie announced that he wanted to go to England the devastation felt by the public was like the aftermath of one, too.

I would have to say, though, that Charlie, in spite of what anyone thinks, did not owe Celtic or the club's supporters one little thing. He cost the club nothing when he came from their unofficial nursery side, Celtic Boys Club, and he made them £750,000 when he eventually moved to Arsenal in 1983. Charlie had broken his leg playing for Celtic's reserve side at Cappielow against Morton one miserable night in January, 1982 and had mercifully come back to be the powerful presence he always was. Charlie was aware, though, that one more accident on that level and his commercial value on the transfer market would seriously diminish. That kind of nagging doubt has the effect of making a player think he might as well get kicked in England for big money as smaller wages in Scotland.

The idea of going south was irresistible to Charlie, therefore it did not matter what kind of improved offer Celtic made to him when his contract was at an end. In fairness to the club, they tried their best to keep him but he was being drawn by a magnet and only the final destination was unclear in his mind. Since I was the one who knew him best at Celtic Park, he came to me like an older brother for advice and I can say now that it was me who told Charlie Nicholas he should sign for Arsenal. There will be those who will look back at the four years Charlie has spent in the English League and the negative effect it has had on his career and tell me that this was the kind of guidance he could have done without, but at the time it was sound reason to my way of thinking.

Charlie, for once in his life, was unsure of himself. There were stories circulating that various people unconnected with Celtic were promised vast sums of money if they could get him to go to clubs other than Arsenal once his contract was up. But I knew Terry Neil, who was then the manager at Highbury, and I respected his views on how the game should be played. As well as that, the other main contenders for Charlie's signature were not suitable to him for vastly different reasons.

The idea of playing beside Kenny Dalglish in the same Liverpool team did not appeal to him for one thing. Kenny had been Charlie's idol as a boy when he supported Celtic, and the notion of going to Anfield seemed to have an intimidating effect on him. It is probably a pity that the opportunity to go to Liverpool did not arise a couple of years later, by which time Kenny was the manager there. He could have been the one to restore Charlie's sense of direction where his career is concerned. In 1983 the idea of going to Liverpool was a non-starter and Manchester United were never quoted, either, once Charlie had a meeting with the man who was then in charge at Old Trafford, Ron Atkinson. They had a secret meeting two days before Scotland were to meet England at Wembley but even Charlie, who was hardly the introverted type, found Ron's image of personal jewellery and champagne a bit too much to take.

It was at that point he took his problems to me. Some might argue that the first thing I should have told him was to sign up with Celtic for another couple of years so that he might mature as a player and a person and then be able to know his own mind better. I can't go along with that because although Charlie had the long hair, the earring and the distinctive dress sense that made him look like a frivolous person, he was in fact a very shrewd operator.

His misfortune was in walking into so much upheaval at Highbury. Terry Neil was sacked and his successor, Don Howe, did not seem to know where best to play Charlie in the team. This was an astonishing state of affairs given that he had scored fifty-three goals in all during his last season at Celtic Park and been awarded the title of Player of the Year, which suggested Charlie might have had a reasonable future playing up front! Now he looks a different player altogether, tactically and physically speaking, since the legs and hips are thicker and the pace is less searing. While he was with Celtic, though, Charlie brought additional quality to a team that was already well off in that respect and at a stage when Scottish football was being well served outside Glasgow, too, by emerging talents. There are no such things as bogey teams or Indian signs: if one side has better players than the other, then they win, and competition was keen.

It is a time I look back on with fond memories. Only six months after my career had been given back to me following the long lay-off with foot trouble I was chosen for Scotland once again. It had seemed that, even if I did manage to play for Celtic once more, my international career would be at an end because it would be asking too much to scale those heights again. To disprove that theory was yet another boost to my morale. To overcome such a worrying period in my life had, generally speaking, a profound effect on me. Perhaps because I had been out of circulation for so long in the social sense while I was in plaster or on crutches, I started to get invited out a lot more, and it was then I learned to unwind and even take a drink while I was relaxing.

I was in my thirties but I knew I was good for a few years more. It was time, then, to enjoy to the full the remainder of my stay in the game, savouring the good and accepting the bad with good grace. With a fractured skull, diabetes and a mysterious injury behind me, I also thought I had lived through the superstitious person's calculation that bad news comes in batches of three. That would turn out to be a mathematical error, but on either side of my next visit to the casualty ward there would be plenty to cram in, including belatedly reaching the pinnacle of my career by adding the title of captain of Scotland after my name.

8

Captain of Scotland

Jock Stein had promised me before he left Celtic Park as manager to take over Leeds United that he would look after me if he ever became the man in charge of Scotland. At the time I did not know what he meant and I could not allow myself to think too much about his words, either, because the forty-three caps I had already won up until 1977 seemed destined to be the figure that would ultimately go against my name in the record books. When I was chosen to play against Belgium at Hampden in December, 1979, even the date of the match made me wonder if I had been selected out of sentiment, as a Christmas bonus for having had the resilience to overcome the disability that had threatened to put an end to my career.

On reflection, and since I made another eighteen appearances for Scotland after that night, I am satisfied in my own mind that charity had nothing to do with it. Confirmation of that for me was being named as captain of Scotland in April 1981 against Israel in a World Cup Qualifying tie. Even the man who had been my greatest influence since I started in the game would not have indulged himself to that degree and I could sense by then that I was improving with every match at domestic and international level.

Regaining my place in the national side had, if anything, increased the pressure on me to maintain a certain standard of performance. Once I had done that, my goal was then to lead the team into the 1982 World Cup finals in Spain. The easy part was playing for Celtic. If a club keeps players of quality, as Celtic did then, the strain on the individual is not so great. We had won the championship in the 1980-81 season by seven points from Aberdeen, strengthened by the inspired signing of Frank McGarvey from Liverpool, and we moved into the next one seemingly ready to be every bit as dominant at home and make a proper go at Europe for the first time in a long while.

The first-round draw put us in with Juventus, and in spite of the frail look about our one-goal lead from the first leg at Celtic Park there was no sense of foreboding before our trip to Italy, especially after beating Rangers at Ibrox the following Saturday. For me, though, the Champions Cup was at an end for another season because I was to break my leg against Partick Thistle a week later. It was an injury so uncomplicated compared to those I had suffered before that I sometimes forget myself that it actually happened to me. In fact, I wasn't even sure at the time that I had been badly hurt. I had gone for the ball with Kenny Watson of Partick Thistle in front of the 'Jungle', but even after I had been treated on the park and it had been decided to substitute me, I still managed to walk halfway round the ground and into the dressing room.

On closer inspection, though, I was back at the Victoria Infirmary, keeping my reputation as one of the hospital's best customers. The team spirit at Celtic Park then was such that it was decided I should go with the European Cup party to Turin in any case, and my memories of that trip are fragrant in every way except for the score. Celtic's headquarters were in a wine-producing region of the country, and since I was there as a first-class tourist I could visit the vineyards whenever I liked in the company of Bobby Lennox, who had been appointed reserve team coach with Celtic by then. If you have to be in plaster, this is the way to enjoy your convalescence!

There were only six weeks of the good life, though, before I returned, free of side effects, and was able to resume my part in helping Celtic win the title, again from Aberdeen, and leading Scotland to Malaga for our first World Cup tie against New Zealand. If anyone wanted proof that Jock Stein was not acting out of soft heartedness when he had me there, the opening match was it. I was directly responsible for donating New Zealand one of the goals they scored that night in June and I was promptly dropped for the next match against Brazil, captain or not.

My last game for Scotland was against Russia, when we had a 2-2 draw and departed the tournament. I had come on as a substitute and when the immediate crushing disappointment had gone I asked Jock Stein for a private discussion. Before the squad returned home I told him that to make it easier for all concerned I considered my time as an internationalist to be at an end and that I did not want to be picked any more. His reaction was to tell me to say nothing to anyone because he was not so sure I had nothing left to offer my country. He asked me not to make anything public because he might want to use my experience in the opening internationals of the following season as he reconstructed the side for the European championships and, beyond that, for the 1986 World Cup finals in Mexico.

Jock was not the kind of man you argued with, but I had not taken the decision lightly and I knew deep down that I did not want that. I had made my statement, if you like, at that level of the game over the sixty-two times I had played for Scotland in the previous ten years. Becoming a full internationalist had made me a better player but I did not want an established reputation to be sullied by going into decline in full view of the spectating public.

The kind of job that Jock Stein wanted me to do in a dark blue jersey I was no longer physically able to do. The overlapping full back was a pleasant memory for me and, hopefully, for the Scotland supporters. As well as that, though, I was being given the opportunity to leave the international stage in surroundings that were memorable: the World Cup and playing against the best in a magnificent stadium. It would have been an anti-climax, to my way of thinking, to bow out by possibly being taken off at Wrexham against Wales or something of that sort. Eventually Jock accepted my point of view and I arrived home with no sense of regret, only deep satisfaction that I had enjoyed such a long and fulfilling addition to my experiences with Celtic. If it should strike anyone as inconsistent that I gave up playing for Scotland in 1982 and yet went on for another five years at Celtic Park in the Premier Division, I can explain.

International football is, quite simply, on a different plane altogether from club level. To mix with players you have only read about is to appreciate that on Scotland assignments. John Robertson, the former Nottingham Forest winger, was a prime example. He was once described by his manager at the time, Brian Clough, as a slovenly tramp. Where Brian was absolutely correct is that it has rarely been my experience to meet a young man who could be wearing a Saville Row suit yet look as if he had been dragged through a hedge backwards, but John Robertson could manage that with ease. I can also remember the dressing room in Malaga at half time during those World Cup matches and John sneaking into the toilet for a quick cigarette!

When the referee's whistle blew, though, he could do things with a ball and manoeuvre that stocky, little frame of his in a way that made him a delight to watch. His type do not come along too often in the Premier Division and that is why I was able to last twenty years with a body of my own that had, to put it mildly, been well lived in. These are the memories I retain from my time with Scotland, along with the nine caps I have at home. Only one cap is given for each year a player has represented his country, no matter whether it has been a

World Cup year or not, which has always struck me as a pity when two jerseys are issued to each team member, one to keep and one to swop with the opposition. I used to have ten caps but I sold one, not, I should add, because I needed the money, but because someone else did.

Prominent footballers are always being asked to involve themselves in charity work. My attitude to that is that it is the least we can do to help out the less fortunate. Players have the time on their hands and, as nobody knows better than me, we should be grateful for our own good health. Most of my efforts are, of course, directed towards charities that help diabetics but wherever possible, I try to make myself available to help out a good cause.

As one who has been in hospital quite a lot, off and on, I know how uplifting it can be, too, to get a visitor. Sometimes, though, it can be a heart-rending business and involve a considerable effort to force yourself through the ward door. The burns unit at Glasgow's Yorkhill Hospital for Sick Children is one such place. I can think back to one day when I visited a boy there who was no more than ten years of age. He had lost an arm as well as his foot after touching an overhead cable on one line of the city's electrified train service, an all too common accident, unfortunately, suffered by many youngsters who are skylarking near their homes.

This particular child was very heavily sedated to help him cope with the pain of his injuries and his parents had been told the rest of his life could possibly be measured in days rather than anything else. Perhaps because no-one wants to accept these things easily, they asked me to have my photograph taken with him, anyway, so that they could prove to him that Danny McGrain had visited him once he had gained full consciousness. A few days later I heard that he had rallied and staged a recovery, and after that came the news that he was out of danger. That boy has since visited me at Celtic Park, using his artificial limbs. His recovery had nothing at all to do with my visit, of course, but the fact that I was able to help in some small way made me feel good. It is a small gesture, but there are other players, like Tommy Burns of Celtic, whose work in that way has made my admiration for them as people, never mind professional footballers, grow.

My international cap went to raise funds to get an artificial arm for another small boy. It was bought by Rod Stewart, who promised £500 for it along with a gold disc for one of his recordings and was as good as his word. The time spent doing this kind of work should never be grudged.

When I was awarded the M.B.E. in 1983, however, it had nothing to do with my small contribution to charity work but was, I am also delighted to say, for services to the game of football. The honours system starts off with an unassuming envelope arriving through the post bearing the name of Downing Street. At first I thought it was an extreme form of tax demand but inside was a letter saying I had been put forward for this particular 'gong' and asking me whether or not I wished to accept the award. There are even boxes at the bottom to be ticked 'Yes' or 'No'. My grateful acceptance was sent off by return post, even though the trip to Buckingham Palace would turn out to cost me a fortune.

I had two excitable daughters to dress up for the occasion and a wife who was due to give birth a matter of days after my investiture and was then fantasising about having the baby in the Queen's official residence and being attended by the royal physician. As you can imagine, excitement was running high, almost as high as the figures on the pocket calculator once I had added the cost of booking a hotel in London and hiring a limousine so that we could arrive at the address at the end of the Mall in a style befitting the occasion.

The hardest part was keeping the news of the award secret from everyone, including my parents, for months on end. It is a nerve-wracking day when it finally dawns, too. You are separated from your guests once inside the Palace and taken upstairs to a room where those who are on the Honours List with you are assembled. There is even a form of class distinction practised here because those who are to be knighted are kept to one side, while the more common Members, Orders and Commanders of the British Empire are moved to the other to be tutored on what to do by a member of the Queen's household staff.

It is what not to do that is the most important thing of all to remember. You must never, for example, speak to the member of the Royal Family officiating at the ceremony until they speak to you first of all, and it is a very definite breach of etiquette to turn your back on the royal personage once your bit is over. Two steps backwards, a quick pivot and then off, that is what I was instructed to do. I waited for my place in the queue and shut my eyes, trying to take it all in and hoping not to do anything that was treasonable. As it turned out, I ended up second last behind an immense line of people and was riddled with nerves by the time my turn came. The Queen was on a royal tour at that time, and so I was given my medal by the Queen Mother. Don't ask me why I remember such a small detail, but I can always recollect that she had a bad cough that day and I had this overwhelming urge to tell her she should take better care of herself.

The actual extent of our conversation was that Her Royal Highness asked me if I still enjoyed playing football, to which I could just about reply that I certainly did. And that was it. The limousine was parked in the forecourt, and after getting the obligatory photographs taken I took the family back to our hotel. It was still only midday, too, so, after receiving the M.B.E. from the Queen Mother at Buckingham Palace, the McGrains did the only thing possible, we went to the pictures!

The 'gong' was placed in the hotel safe, the top hat and tails went into the wardrobe and we went off to see *Dark Crystal.* I can never forget that because Dawn, who is my accident-prone daughter, tripped over while walking upstairs to the balcony and sent the contents of her carton of coke showering down on a poor, unsuspecting customer for the stalls. If I had told him why we were all a bit on edge that day, he would never have believed me.

The experience was one never to be forgotten, the Palace not the pictures, I mean, and it was a time in my life when I found myself being introduced to various, previously unsampled events. The captaincy of Scotland was one and, less enjoyably, getting sent off was another. It happened to me playing against Aberdeen at Celtic Park on October 9, 1982 and will always rank as one of the regrets I will have when I look back on my playing career. The match referee, Andrew Waddell from Edinburgh, was one of those very officious people for whom there is no such thing as two sides to an argument, only his view. I had been booked in the first half of the match for a foul on Peter Weir, which was a gross miscarriage of justice in my eyes. When I committed another foul on the same player after the interval I could see by the look on his face that Mr. Waddell was going to show me the red card.

I was outraged because I felt I had not deserved the first booking and yet, here I was, being dismissed for basically committing one rash tackle in the whole of a demanding league game in front of almost thirty thousand people. It would have to happen at the side of the pitch furthest away from the tunnel, of course, and I felt embarrassed and humiliated as I made my way off. By then I had been fifteen years with Celtic and I had been hoping that, however long I lasted and whoever I was playing for, I would never know the sensation of being sent for an early bath. It never happened again after that, so I suppose one indiscretion in twenty years can hardly be considered the record of a villain on the park.

To be sent off at that precise moment was all the more frustrating, though, because it came immediately after one of the finest European results Celtic had achieved in modern times, when we went to Amsterdam and beat the world-renowned Ajax, complete with Johann Cruyff, Jesper Olsen, Jan Molby and Soren Lerby, on their own ground.

It was in the first round of the European Cup and was a tie that contradicted all the ground rules that are supposed to be followed if a team is to make sustained progress in that competition. For one thing we played the first leg at home and failed to win, which is supposedly the equivalent of signing your own death warrant! Within four minutes of the start in the game at Celtic Park, Jesper Olsen, one of the fastest and nimblest players I have ever come across, waltzed through our defence, myself included, and put the Dutchmen in front. Although Charlie Nicholas equalised, we always seemed to be chasing the game and Lerby put Ajax in front again just to confirm our worst fears. Frank McGarvey eventually cancelled that one out, too, however, and all this happened inside the first half-hour to prove it wasn't a bad game to watch.

Given such a score to take to Holland, Celtic were thought to require a miracle to go through to the next round, especially since longevity in European competition was no longer the club's strong suit. In all the years I had been playing at that level for Celtic up until then we had failed to get as far as, or beyond, the second round of any of the three major competitions in seven out of twelve attempts.

An even bigger crowd than had watched us in Glasgow, over 65,000, watched the return leg. This is theoretically the game in which a club in Celtic's position plays in a highly cautious manner and hopes that the age of miracles has not passed. Instead, we went for the jugular and found ourselves a goal ahead on aggregate after thirty-five minutes when Charlie Nicholas and Frank McGarvey constructed a thing of beauty which Charlie finished off. The legendary Johann Cruyff, idol of the people, was, meanwhile, being totally shut out of the game by Graeme Sinclair. He had been signed by Billy McNeill the month before from Dumbarton, a part-time side, costing the kind of money that would not have been enough to meet Cruyff's tax bill for the year, and had not been at Celtic Park long enough to memorise his dressing-room peg number. I have always believed that when Cruyff went off that night, to be substituted by Molenaar, he was using the fact that Ajax had equalised with twenty-five minutes to go through Vanenburg to stage a diplomatic retreat and cover up for the fact that he had hardly got a kick at the ball.

The result as it stood in the dying minutes was level on aggregate but enough to take Ajax through on the away goals rule. With just two minutes left, though, George McCluskey created and scored the goal that won Celtic a distinguished victory and allowed us to temporarily delude ourselves that we were capable of reviving the club's illustrious past in Europe.

It was naive of us to think so, but then our naivety had carried us through in the first place against the odds and contrary to all logic. By the time we were put up against Real Sociedad of Spain in round two we were back to the conventional approach and paying the opposition just enough respect to hang ourselves instead of them. In the first leg on their pitch we played a containing game that is always alien to any Celtic side, but we almost got away with it. Two goals within the space of four minutes, and the first of them with only quarter of an hour to go, only proved once again that very nearly is not good enough, however. At Celtic Park we reverted to type in order to make up the leeway and then fell victim to what can occasionally happen under these circumstances: the opposition scored before we did. Two goals from Murdo Macleod won the match on the night but that is a worthless distinction over two legs.

In the space of two rounds Celtic had shown that we were capable only of being schizophrenic in Europe, but the only way of correcting that kind of collective defect in a team is by getting plenty of practice at that level. The vicious circle principle means that the club cannot stay in any competition long enough to attain that experience because we have only once gone by the second round in the four seasons that have followed on from that defeat by the Spaniards.

Having been lucky enough to possess such a talented and spirited side, though, in domestic competition, what was lost on the continent was quickly compensated for at home. The month after losing to Real Sociedad, Celtic beat Rangers in the final of the League Cup. It would turn out to be the only trophy the club would get that season but at the same time it allowed Billy McNeill to maintain his average of having at least one prize to show for each of the five seasons that he had been manager at Celtic Park.

He seemed to sense in me, too, that I was still keen to make up for lost time where my playing career was concerned. When my contract ended that summer, he offered me fresh terms with Celtic, knowing I had no interest at that point in coaching or management. I accepted them readily. Even if Charlie Nicholas' move to England, which happened at the same time, was inevitable, the manager had always played the transfer market very wisely, and when he signed a promising young player called Brian McClair from Motherwell there seemed to be no reason why Billy McNeill could not continue to bring the club and its supporters what they had come to expect, which was a team who played with flair and had a passionate will to win as well as the right level of nerve for the big occasion. Ten days after Brian McClair's arrival, though, Billy McNeill was no longer Celtic's manager but the man in charge of Manchester City at Maine Road after one of the most inglorious chapters in the club's history.

9

Billy McNeill and David Hay

Celtic rewrote the club's history when they removed David Hay from managerial office and replaced him with Billy McNeill on May 28, 1987. It was also a radical step that had to be taken to improve the club's decaying public image.

There has been no one issue that has divided the supporters of Celtic from the people who run the club more than the sacking of Billy McNeill in the summer of 1983. It was not officially termed dismissal, but it was the sack by any other name. Billy had publicly voiced his disappointment that, in spite of his creditable record as manager, the board at Celtic Park had never seen fit in five years to put him on a contract, far less give him the wage rise that would give him an annual salary in keeping with the status that his job carried.

It was clearly a ploy on his part to force the directors into recognising his worth but it was construed as a threat instead and a formal statement was issued denying his request, as it was called, for improved terms and conditions. For a proud man like Billy McNeill this was tantamount to being told that he was not wanted any more at Celtic Park, thereby making it impossible for him to stay any longer. Within a matter of days he was on his way to Manchester City where his managerial qualities would be appreciated.

When I was asked by reporters at the time for my views on what had taken place I was openly critical of the club, and nothing has happened in the intervening years to make me alter my opinion. It was a despicable act by Celtic because Billy McNeill was a man with a family to support like anybody else and he was more than entitled to think he was due better treatment. It was also a difficult time for him in his private life because the property business that he had helped form away from football had collapsed, involving a severe financial loss on his part.

I will never forget breaking the news to him of that misfortune a year earlier. Celtic were on a pre-season trip to West Germany and one night, when I had telephoned home, Laraine had told me that the company had folded. We were shocked because I had invested some money in the business, too, but Billy was left devastated by the revelation.

Apart from those purely financial considerations, though, the directors were wrong to abuse one of the club's legendary figures. To many people Billy McNeill was – still is – Celtic. He gave the club twenty-five years of his life, and their history, as player and manager, and there are some supporters, I know, who are now preparing to go back and watch the team play for the first time since that whole, regrettable episode. They were the ones who always carried around this mental image of Billy standing alone on a rostrum in the Estadio Nacional in Lisbon in 1967 with the European Cup held above his head, or could still clearly see him rising above the Dunfermline defence to score the winning goal in the Scottish Cup final two years previously in the game that brought Celtic out of the wilderness of eight barren years without a single trophy. Celtic were his life, which was probably his undoing in the first place.

When Celtic were looking for a manager to replace Jock Stein, they were obviously in a very difficult position. After all, how do you follow a genius? Desperate as they were, however, Billy gave the impression of being even more desperate to manage Celtic. He said himself at the time that it was a case of his heart ruling his head in taking the decision to leave Aberdeen, where he had been for only a year but had quickly become a greatly respected figure. That was when he made his first mistake, and the club took full advantage of his fanaticism, which is a commodity they like to play on in lieu of wages.

He should have insisted on becoming the first manager at Celtic Park ever to have a contract. The club have always employed this tradition that they hire men to run the side on the basis of a gentleman's agreement. Tradition has its place but it is in a museum. It is certainly not worth much in the game of football in this day and age.

Celtic's outlook baffles me even more because a written agreement is a safeguard for them as well as the man who is their manager. Contracts can be terminated as easily as they can be extended if all is going well, and if all the players have one, how can it be wrong to extend the manager the same courtesy? So far as Billy McNeill's wages were concerned, it was nothing short of scandalous that the manager of Celtic should be paid less than his counterparts at clubs like Aberdeen and Dundee United. In the time he was at Celtic Park, Billy watched both those sides win the Premier Division championship and other major honours under Alex Ferguson and Jim McLean. What they achieved in taking on the Old Firm was astonishing and he would not have denied either man his money, no matter how much it was. Nor would he have objected to whatever John Greig was earning over the corresponding period with Rangers, even though there could be little doubt which half of the Old Firm had the more successful manager.

It was the idea of being fourth in the earnings table when he was with one half of that historic Old Firm, with all the burdens of that responsibility, that angered him, however, and rightly so. In the dressing room the opinion of the players was that, as with Jock Stein before him, Celtic would be a successful club for as long as he remained at the helm. He was not a saint but an ordinary man with the most basic faults. However, he was an arch motivator of men who was building a Celtic side with the devotion that he brought to everything connected with the club. A lot of Celtic's natural confidence went away when he was forced to leave the club, and the recriminations that followed, which descended to some pretty messy levels, made matters worse. There were revelations about a private financial transaction between the board and the manager, and the ill feeling this caused among supporters, as well as the level of sympathy for Billy McNeill, must have surprised the directors.

For one thing, they had been shown, yet again, to have very little sense of style. If the board of directors all drove up to Celtic Park one morning in a fleet of Rolls Royces I think the ordinary follower of the club would find that more acceptable than the penny-pinching image Celtic have in the eyes of the public, where Rangers are portrayed as *Dynasty* while Celtic represent *Coronation Street.* The board should have been big enough to know that when Billy McNeill aired his grievances in public it was with the intention of challenging Celtic to come into the twentieth century in their dealings with employees and to make them discuss his problems on a businesslike level. The fact that they took the course of action they did, on the other hand, encouraged us all to think that they wanted Billy McNeill off the premises.

It is, thankfully, an account now settled in time for the club's centenary year, albeit with some outstanding details to be taken care of, such as the production of the contract for Billy McNeill the directors now say he can have. His return has restored Billy as the head of the Celtic family, a role reinforced in the minds of the supporters who showed the depth of their affection for him with that moving reception before the one hundredth Scottish Cup final, when he was introduced to the crowd beforehand and almost brought the proceedings to a standstill.

His enforced move to Manchester meant a bad time for the club, in any case, as everybody tried to come to terms with what had taken place. David Hay, one of my own playing contemporaries, was appointed manager, but how he could have taken on the job without a contract after all the controversy surrounding Billy McNeill surprised me greatly. So did the fact that he accepted the job after he had been told that Frank Connor, a board appointment, would be his assistant.

Let me make it clear that I have nothing personal against Frank Connor. He is a great enthusiast and his commitment to Celtic could never be doubted. The relationship between any manager and his assistant, though, has to be based on a certain chemistry between the two men, and Frank and David belonged to two different generations. That is not to say that the players ever witnessed any arguments between the two of them, because we did not, which was in contrast to Billy McNeill and John Clark, but it was a partnership that was obviously doomed to failure, and that created another unnecessary diversion along an already hard road.

David Hay always goes his own way, though. The last time we met before he walked through the door as manager at Celtic Park was in Clearwater, Florida when he had taken his family on holiday to the United States at the same time as the McGrains were there. He had never given me the impression that he was anxious for a managerial career in Scotland, and although he had enjoyed a very entertaining season in charge of Motherwell, eventually winning them promotion to the Premier Division, he had resigned in the hope of going back to live in America on a permanent basis. In other words, David had been out of the game completely for a year before taking over Celtic.

He came in quietly and his temperament has never changed at all in the years that have passed since then. It is not, as people might think, that David Hay is a serious-minded person. Thinking back to our days together in the Celtic youth team of the sixties, I can remember on our first continental trip to Casale Monferrato, in Italy, the young David driving a scooter in between the tables in a pavement cafe and passing out the other side like a stunt man in a film. I don't know whether it happened by accident or design but he certainly looked as if he was enjoying himself. He knows how to laugh all right, but it would have been easy, for a couple of reasons, to get the wrong idea about him as he settled into the job of managing Celtic.

First of all, people might have thought he was basically an unlucky person, which is definitely not a welcome trait in a manager. Since the day and hour David left Celtic in 1974 (after a disagreement over money, which nobody will be surprised to hear!), his life seemed to fall apart. The Hay family went on holiday to Cyprus and a civil war broke out. An injury to his retina then almost cost him his sight in one eye, and his playing career was prematurely ended by a severe injury to his knee while at Chelsea. Even his failure to get the necessary documentation from the immigration authorities in order to enter the United States helped fit the identikit picture of the unfortunate person.

In his first full season at Celtic Park the team lost in the final of the League Cup and in the Scottish Cup as well, finishing up in second place in the Premier Division championship, all of which hardly contradicted that theory. For such a quiet and reserved man, too, some of David's outbursts in the press landed him with an undeserved reputation for being a bad loser. The truth is that he could probably have done with losing his temper more often, especially in the dressing room, but he was not the victim of paranoia that he was made out to be.

The misconceptions started to grow up, however, on the day that Aberdeen defeated Celtic in the Scottish Cup final at Hampden in 1984. Roy Aitken was sent off for a foul on Mark McGhee, who would ultimately go on to score the winning goal in extra time. It was one of those days where a ten-man Celtic side battled in epic fashion to make the numerical disadvantage look as if it were actually working in our favour, only to end up with a bad case of glorious failure on our hands. At the end, probably carried away with the highly charged and emotional atmosphere, David went into the press room at Hampden and was very critical of the S.F.A. secretary, Ernie Walker.

The secretary had visited the Celtic dressing room before the game started and delivered a talk on the subject of violent conduct on the park, apparently because of tension in previous games between Aberdeen and ourselves. It was certainly an unusual step to take in my experience and Celtic, as a club, felt that Mr Walker's actions had intensified the pressure on the match referee, Bob Valentine from Dundee.

Considering that we had also lost the League Cup final to Rangers in extra time and had departed the U.E.F.A. Cup in the third round because our team could not match Nottingham Forest for tactical

As a best man they don't come any better than Kenny Dalglish. Has a tendency to overdo his responsibilities, however!

Another shot from the family album, attending the wedding of a supporter who later named his first born after me. Luckily it was a boy!

The Golden Boot presented to me by the Celtic supporters on May 25, 1987. It will take pride of place in our house for me, Dawn (top left), Vicki (top right), Carly (centre) and my wife Laraine.

Whether the working clothes are hooped

or dark blue, timing and passing are all important.

What the well
dressed player
was wearing in
1983 before
he went to the
Palace to be
awarded the
M.B.E.

This picture shows the camera can be deceptive sometimes. Hurdling an opponent from Ibrox without hurting him.

At the end of it all, memories. Saluting the fans after the League Championship had been won in 1977.

Showing the Scottish Cup to a packed house before my testimonial match against Manchester United in 1980.

My only regret is I never got the chance to say goodbye like this to the people who make Celtic what they really are.

The last hurrah. The final medal I won as a Celtic player was the League Championship taken on the last day of the 1985-86 season at Love Street.

awareness, it was easy to believe a state of decline was in progress. There then followed one of the most bizarre episodes in Celtic's history, and one that implied things were going to get far worse before they got better. In David Hay's second season in charge we played in the Cup Winners Cup because Aberdeen had also won the championship. This is normally considered a fair consolation prize to the losing finalists at Hampden, but it turned out to be no kind of favour at all to Celtic. After beating Ghent of Belgium in the first round, Celtic were drawn against Rapid Vienna, whose name will be forever synonymous with cheating, arrogance and generally unpleasant memories for our supporters.

The Austrians' treatment of us on their own pitch, and the leniency of the match officials, were questionable to say the least. Frank McGarvey was badly hurt after a vicious tackle yet he was not allowed treatment. His place had to be taken eventually by Alan McInally, who was then sent off for his first, innocuous tackle of the match. This saw to it that Celtic would be two men down for the return leg because I was booked for something so trivial I can't even remember what it was and had that added to a caution from earlier in the season in the same tournament, meaning I was automatically suspended for one game.

The return leg turned out to be the infamous night when Rapid Vienna came close to bringing anarchy to the game by threatening to walk off the pitch at Celtic Park, and we took a step towards depriving ourselves of our own good name on the continent. The 3-1 aggregate lead that Rapid brought to Glasgow flattered them, since Celtic had played very well under trying circumstances in Austria and had only conceded the last goal three minutes from the end there, which is always a frustrating experience. We were all square again by half time at Celtic Park, though, because of goals from Brian McClair and Murdo MacLeod. The Rapid players had lost the place by then as a result of Celtic demonstrating the kind of inspired form that we rarely managed to achieve in a European context, and one of them, Keinast, was sent off after the interval for an incident off the ball with Tommy Burns. Before that Tommy had put Celtic in front for the first time in the tie, though Rapid protested that he had fouled the goalkeeper in the process.

When the obviously flustered goalkeeper, Ehn, then aimed a deliberate kick at the same Celtic player, it sparked off a lengthy discussion between the referee, his linesman and most of the by now demented Rapid players. Unfortunately, the referee decided to hold this forum in front of the 'Jungle' for fully fifteen minutes, during which time the patience of an exasperated fan ran out and a bottle was thrown on to the pitch. This was like tossing a match towards sweating dynamite, as the Austrians immediately enacted a mime in which one of them, Weinhofer, went down holding his head and the rest ran to the scene of the supposed crime with concern written all over their faces. From where I was sitting in the stand I was satisfied that nothing had touched Weinhofer, and television evidence afterwards corroborated that view.

I am not saying that a missile thrown on to the park should be dismissed as high spirits just because it fails to reach its intended target but Rapid seized upon that incident as their chance to stay in Europe where their efforts on the field had not been enough to keep them in the competition by legitimate means.

Weinhofer, who did not have a mark on him from what I could see inside the pavilion afterwards, had his head dressed in bandages in a way that left him looking like a cross between a man in a turban and an Egyptian mummy as he left the ground. We should have known there and then we would never hear the end of the matter, but equally Celtic should have acted in a more principled manner in the weeks that followed.

After the first disciplinary hearing held by the governing body of football in Europe, U.E.F.A., Celtic seemed to be exonerated in that we were only fined £4,000 because a bottle was thrown inside our premises. The decision to deduct £5,000 from Rapid Vienna for their misbehaviour on the field and to ban their coach for three European matches was a further indication of how the blame for what happened was being apportioned. The claim that Weinhofer was struck by a bottle was dismissed, too, giving us mixed feelings of relief and vindication. The Austrians' decision to appeal against the findings of the disciplinary committee should have been Celtic's cue to pull out of the tournament with our pride intact.

The modern-day footballer is not supposed to be a particularly highly principled individual but I can assure you that the mood in the Celtic dressing room at that time was that it was better to withdraw with dignity than to put up with watching natural justice being tampered with, as we did while the rest of the sordid story unfolded. Celtic were represented at the appeal hearing by one of our directors, Jimmy Farrell, who is a member of the legal profession, and yet the club accepted the original verdict being completely overturned by a committee that was apparently well short of its full complement, with some members later reporting that they were unaware it was even taking place.

At the hearing, medical evidence was also submitted, and accepted, where it would be rejected as inadmissible in another case some months later, and Celtic were ordered to play the second leg over again at least one hundred miles from our own ground. The fact that the club had compromised themselves was inexcusable, and to say that these arrangements were being agreed to because the Celtic players wanted their chance to go through fairly and squarely on the field of play without concerning ourselves with internal politics is simply not true.

The very least that should have been agreed to was a sudden-death play-off with the aggregate score forgotten about. Being made to start two goals down was only adding insult to multiple injury. A purely personal opinion is that Celtic agreed to the match because it was an extremely lucrative proposition. The club had made good money from the game with Rapid in Glasgow which was watched by almost 50,000 people and they knew that as commercial ventures went the third meeting, which was to be held at the Celtic supporters' favourite ground in England, Old Trafford, would be irresistible to the paying public, and so it turned out to be.

There were even more people in the North of England than there had been in the East End of Glasgow to watch the match because there is nothing that gets the average Celtic supporter more worked up than a sense of injustice against his team. The emotional overkill was just too much to take on the night for the players, though, and all the club succeeded in doing was to bring even more discredit upon Celtic as two Austrian players were attacked by supporters during and after a match which they won by the only goal. In the end, Celtic got what they asked for, a fine of £17,000 and an order to play our next European tie behind closed doors at Celtic Park.

It was, in effect, another huge blow to the club in the financial sense as well as a fatal strike against our prospects of going on in whatever competition we next played in, because the players were being asked to take on the opposition with one hand tied behind our backs. It would have been hard to imagine a more depressing sequence of events, except that the club was lifted out of its self-pitying mood by another remarkable occurrence, the signing of Maurice Johnston from Watford. For Celtic to break the Scottish transfer record as it stood then and pay Watford £450,000 for a player whose style had gripped the imagination of the public in both

Scotland and England by the time he was twenty-one years old was a startling departure from normal, conservative practice and had an inspiring effect on the rest of the staff.

The irony would be that, even with Maurice Johnston, Celtic would stagger unsteadily on our feet towards our first major honour under David Hay, and without ever demonstrating any of the fresh impetus Mo had brought to the club. Consider a Scottish Cup run that began with Celtic needing a goal four minutes from the end to get us into the second round at the expense of a First Division side, Hamilton Accies. If Inverness Thistle, from the Highland league, gave us predictably less trouble in the next game, which we won by six clear goals at Celtic Park as the team drew its breath for the more serious business to come, the next two stages were once again ordeals.

We needed the assistance of extra time against Dundee in the quarter finals and the same again when Motherwell took a stubborn turn at Hampden in the penultimate round. Somehow, though, we limped into the historic one hundredth Scottish Cup final to meet Dundee United, and if ever there was an occasion when the Celtic supporters deserved to see their team win a match, this was it. They brought more of a sense of Celtic's tradition in these matters to Hampden than we did, and in the end it overwhelmed Dundee United (who had never won the cup before) and their much smaller band of supporters. In spite of the fact that Celtic played poorly, went a goal down just after half time and were going nowhere in particular during the remainder of the match for all that we had used both our substitutes, the crowd stayed with us. It felt as if they were trying to suck the ball into the net for us as we played towards the Celtic end at Hampden.

This exercise in the collective will of the people prevailing over what had looked like the logical outcome, a win for Dundee United, took tangible shape in the game's last quarter of an hour. Davie Provan gained us an equaliser from a free kick that could not have been repeated by him if he had been put under hypnosis. The ball spun in flight in a way that was unusual, as if it were taking two bends instead of one, and then curled in at Hamish McAlpine's left-hand post by what must have been no more than a millimetre.

If that caused the Celtic players to suspect that we were fated to win the trophy, giving life to the old saying that our name was written on it, then Frank McGarvey's goal six minutes from the end brought the undeniable proof that this was the case. Roy Aitken had covered every blade of Hampden's grass that afternoon and his cross was made to look as if it were being guided on to Frank's head as he propelled his body towards the ball and left the Dundee United players looking at each other in resignation and bewilderment. The winning of the Scottish Cup in such a genuinely dramatic fashion proved beyond doubt that David Hay had not been born unlucky, and he would underline that fact with an even more audacious triumph before any of us were very much older. With Celtic, though, the only thing you can expect is the unusual, and so nobody could have felt let down, except the player himself, when it was announced that Frank McGarvey was to be made available for transfer a matter of three days after Hampden.

In the interests of balance, I would have to say that I did not join in the condemnation of that decision, and Frank is a player I have a lot of respect for. I could understand the reasoning behind Celtic's move. They had persevered with Frank during the lengthy part of the season in which he had not played well and then accepted what they thought was a fair price for him after St. Mirren had shown enough initiative to come for one of the game's characters.

It would not be right or fair to criticise the club all of the time, and in that particular instance I don't believe Celtic could be faulted if they felt Frank had run his course on their behalf. As a club, however, Celtic tend to encourage extreme reactions, both of praise and criticism, and on the eve of their Centenary year they will arouse all manner of emotions.

10

The People's Club

Celtic will arrive at their one hundredth birthday and at the crossroads of the club's life at the same time in 1988. The side who were formed out of charitable concern will then have to adopt a more self-seeking, businesslike approach or face the consequences. Their noble background will be captured forever on the pages of the club's history but they will be as impoverished as the people they were brought into being to help unless that change is made. The poor of the East End of Glasgow will, by the twenty-first century, come to mean Celtic and not the nineteenth-century urchins they saved unless the club reverts from its status as a private, limited company to a public concern that allows the supporters of the team to finance a better future in the next hundred years.

Morality does not come into it since the club's contributions to charity are now hardly on the scale they once were, but the admittedly less appealing human trait of envy should be what drives the present board of directors towards the floor of the stock market. Rangers have spent money on a scale that could not have been dreamt of in Scotland until they were bankrolled by the Lawrence Building Group a couple of years ago. Until some other club accepts the need to challenge Rangers and all their wealth – and if that club is not Celtic, who else can anybody look to? – then the game in this country will turn into a monopoly and the spectating public will gradually grow tired of every competition being a foregone conclusion and withdraw their support.

It is no longer good enough for those in control at Celtic Park to stay out of the argument by saying that their club cannot compete at that financial level. They have to investigate ways of maintaining the Old Firm rivalry, rather than being the one half of the partnership that pleads poverty all of the time. Employing Billy McNeill is a good start.

It is also well known among Celtic's support that there are plenty of people in the city of Glasgow who would gladly help out if the club went public. They come from various walks of life, from professional men to self-made businessmen, and they could, given the opportunity, bring about the revolution it will take to help Celtic before it is too late.

If I were asked to put a figure on the amount of money required, I would say it would take ten million pounds in order to run Rangers all the way for supremacy, on and off the field. This sum would include a fund to restore the ground, Celtic Park, that has become a monument to a bygone age. It is a source of embarrassment to the Celtic support, the butt of jokes for everyone else who visits the place. Why it was not renovated twenty years ago, when Celtic were the biggest club in Britain, is beyond me, but the omissions of the past are not as important now as the solutions for the future. On a practical level, the terracings behind each goal should be brought in tight on the byeline and made all-seated. This would increase the atmosphere inside the ground for players and spectators alike as well as take away that vast look of a mausoleum that can distract a player when the crowd is only a fraction of Celtic's present capacity. Better to have 20,000 people in a ground that can hold 40,000 than the same number inside the stadium in its present, bloated form.

The legendary 'Jungle' opposite the main stand would, in my type of structure, be permitted to stay in its original, untouched state. The place is a shrine for those who always go there, no matter who Celtic are playing. Apart from the ones who like to stand in that atmospheric spot, though, I do not believe that the majority expect other than adequate seating arrangements in this day and age. The trouble with Celtic, however, is that the club needs to come under sustained attack before anything, no matter how small, gets done.

I remember the dressing rooms were only refurbished a short time ago after a formal protest by the first-team players to the management. Visitors to the park who are taken on a conducted tour of the ground's interior are usually taken aback by the size of the changing rooms. The players, on the other hand, do not mind how small they are. In a way the echoes of the past can be heard all the more clearly when you look around at the intimate surroundings in which Jimmy McGrory, Patsy Gallagher, Charlie Tully and Jock Stein sat. What we objected to was using the same towels as they did. That is an exaggeration, of course, but the dressing rooms had fallen into a state of disrepair and nothing would have happened unless enough noise had been made.

That, in microcosm, could sum up what will need to happen to force the club on to the open market. Since 1888 the Celtic board has, in the main, been made up of the heirs to three separate dynasties, the Kellys, the Whites and the Grants, all of whose families have a representative on the current board of directors. It is felt, so far as I understand it, that this maintains a close-knit, family atmosphere inside Celtic Park. Interlopers are not welcome and the idea of people buying shares in the club is anathema because the place would then be overrun by entrepreneurial types who would have no respect for the Celtic way of doing things and would completely change the character, not to say the name and the jerseys, of the team. All of that I reject totally out of hand.

There are those who are sufficiently well funded to bring Celtic kicking and screaming into the twentieth century who are also longstanding supporters of the club, alarmed by what they see as a growing acceptance of second best. They would no sooner change the identity of the team than they would their own names by deed poll. But even if they did, and did away with the hooped jerseys at the same time, what difference would it make if the most successful team in Scotland emerged from the other end of the transformation?

The last time Celtic won the Premier League championship, the team were wearing lime green, self-coloured strips on one of the truly remarkable days in the club's history. Did that make a bit of difference to anybody's enjoyment of the occasion? A change must come because tradition alone will not sustain Celtic in the climate of increased competition that exists in this country, and every year lost will make it less likely that they ever catch up.

The benefits Rangers derive from spending literally millions of pounds on new players will go beyond the instant success they are having just now. They have abandoned all thoughts of bringing in their own young players while the club comes back from the wilderness years, but that is not to say there will be no youth programme in operation at Ibrox. In fact their reserve players will, over the next few years, improve substantially because they will only train with, and learn from, the very best men in their profession. That was the kind of background I had in the game, working from an early age with the Celtic team that won the European Cup in 1967. Out of that environment also grew Celtic players like Kenny Dalglish, Lou Macari, George Connolly and David Hay himself to uphold the club's position at the forefront of the game in Scotland. For history to repeat itself, Celtic will need to buy players of a similar stature to Terry Butcher and Chris Woods of Rangers.

That is not to say buy for buying's sake. We all assume that the club are sensible enough not to do that, but Celtic need to be lifted out of themselves by imaginative purchases who will increase the club's standing and encourage others to come and join something forward-looking. Then Celtic's youngsters can be taught better habits by those people and someone like Tommy Craig.

His appointment as first-team coach has been one of the smartest moves Celtic have made in recent years because Tommy is a first-rate coach and thinker on the game. I freely admit he is also a personal friend of mine, but since I might not have considered it outwith the realms of possibility that I could have got that job at the same time as Tommy beat me to it in February 1987, this unsolicited testimonial could come under the heading of it being no loss what a friend gets. Taking on a proper coach, complete with all the sought-after S.F.A. credentials and the full backing of the men from Park Gardens, since Tommy Craig was on the national side's staff at the time, is an intriguing move by Celtic. The club's accepted style of play has often given the supporters the firm conviction that the last thing the team has ever wanted was a theorist about the place.

Celtic play it from the heart, or off the cuff. Whatever you care to call it, they try never to lose sight of the fact that the game of football is a sport and as such is there to be enjoyed. That is why when Celtic play in Europe and attempt to go for a containing game the ball invariably ends up travelling back the way towards the goalkeeper. The team cannot get used to playing in a fixed, tactical pattern. That is why Frank McGarvey always struck me as being the archetypal Celtic player. He didn't know what he was going to do next, so how could any of his team-mates guess ahead of him? Somehow it all worked out and the fans loved it.

It will take time for Tommy Craig to instil a more professional outlook, but he will succeed and respect the wishes of the supporters at the same time. In the end, too, they have to be given a side that is as good as the people who support it. I would have to say that the Celtic support were, and still are, very special to me. Jock Stein used to sum up the Old Firm supporters in this way: when Rangers had a good result and you congratulated one of their followers, he would say, 'What's it got to do with you?' When you said the same thing to a Celtic man, he asked you what you wanted to drink.

Basic good nature has always accompanied support for Celtic, I have found. It may also be true that, at its most fundamental level, support for Celtic is seen as adherence to Catholicism among the club's diehards who go back to the team's formation by a priest in aid of three parishes in the East End of Glasgow. I would hope that the people who hold the club dear to their hearts would not allow that aspect of the club's background to prevent them seeing the whole picture. When people illustrate Celtic's good name by saying that the club has a non-denominational policy of signing Catholic and Protestant players, I know it is done to offer the strongest possible contrast with Rangers and their unwritten rule about not signing people of a certain religious persuasion. How is that supposed to make the non-Catholic players, like myself, feel, however?

We are not men from the moon but simply players who came willingly to Celtic. People like Bertie Peacock in the fifties, Bertie Auld in the sixties, Kenny Dalglish in the seventies and myself over two complete decades did not go on to captain the side and involve ourselves in moments of high achievement because we were trying to prove that a Protestant would try his best for the Catholic team. Celtic did not exactly take us off the streets. We were there because we were good players, or, in the case of Jock Stein, a truly great manager. I would not like to see the day when supporters lost sight of that fact. Everybody at Celtic Park pulls together to provide a united, winning team regardless of what schools the separate individuals went to. The religious base of the club will never change, but integration does no harm to the cause of Celtic, and that would apply as much to the board room, I'm sure, if the doors of the ground were thrown open in order to accommodate the growing need for the men to provide a new direction.

As I have already said, the club are inclined to let acceptable standards slip unless they are forced to see what is right and what is wrong. Another small example was the way in which League championship medals were distributed. These souvenirs are not easily come by, since it takes ten months of playing against all kinds of adversity to decide who gets them. Celtic's way of handing them out, though, used to be that the manager would stand at the front of the bus on the road to an away match at the start of the following season and shout out the names of the players after he had opened boxes to read what was engraved on each medal. The box was then launched in the general direction of the person concerned. This was the presentation ceremony. It was not until the League was won in season 1985-86 that a proper function was organised in a Glasgow hotel.

These small touches can mean a lot to players, as the club's lack of attention to minute detail can give rise to offence. It was the players, for instance, and not the club who organised a special presentation for our long-serving masseur, Jimmy Steele, on his seventieth birthday, by which time he had been with Celtic for thirty-five years. If this should read like a general criticism of the board of directors at Celtic Park, I make no apology for that. It should not always be considered heresy to say anything negative about the club, otherwise nothing would ever get done. The only man I would exclude from blame would be the chairman, Jack McGinn. In my experience he has always been a hard worker for the club and an approachable person into the bargain. My opinion of the rest changed at the time when I was leaving Celtic to become manager of Airdrie one ill-fated day in May of 1986.

When I went into Celtic Park, it was to collect my boots, say my goodbyes and bring to an end what had then been a nineteen-year-long association with the only senior club I had played for.

It was the close season and therefore the ground was empty of players, but the directors were all well aware of the fact that I was going. David Hay came in to wish me well and to offer any practical help he could once I had taken over at Broomfield, which was much appreciated. I went to the boot room, collected what was mine and said cheerio to the women who organise the cleaning and supervision of the kit for the players. But I walked out of the front door at Celtic Park, believing it was for the last time, without a single director coming in to see me and bid me farewell. The critical response to this usually goes along the lines of, well, Celtic gave you a testimonial match. What more do you want? I do not want to sound ungrateful, but on these nights the player being honoured pays for everything out of his cheque for long service. Out of my testimonial money in 1980 came Manchester United's expenses and everything else down to the payment for the ambulance staff on the night of the match. The club give you the hire of their ground for nothing, that is all.

But that is not what I am concerned about at all. To put it into perspective, I was not looking for the directors to break down and weep because one of the longstanding members of the team was going away. I had always believed, like the supporters, that there was a family atmosphere at the club, though. In that case, why did no-one turn up when the oldest boy was leaving the homestead?

In future, I will go back to Celtic Park to watch the development of players I have worked beside, but I will pay my own way into the ground to see the matches rather than be hypocritical and ask for a complimentary ticket from one of the directors. It is unlikely I would get past the doorman at Celtic Park, in any case, since we fell out on the night of Roy Aitken's testimonial match, which also happened to be against Manchester United.

I had gone in the company of my mother and father, who avidly followed my career as a Celtic player from day one with the club. They went in ahead of me while I stopped to talk to a couple of supporters. When I eventually got to the front door, the commissionaire refused to let me pass until I had shown him my parents' tickets. And I was still the captain of the club at the time! I was so angry at having to fumble in my pocket for the tickets that once I had found them and proved we were not trying to sneak in I went straight to the chairman and made an official complaint. Hopefully the club will sort out their public relations because it is a pity to part company with Celtic and have any kind of unpleasant memories.

The more wholesome side of the story is that, in twenty years at Celtic Park, I can honestly say I have never come across anyone, from the playing staff to the maintenance men who work around the ground, that I have ever disliked. There will always be emotional ties and these will extend to the members of my own family, in spite of my being surrounded by women.

One of my daughters, Vicki, is a real football fan who actually knows the laws of the game and takes more than a passing interest in the personalities involved. Her favourite players, according to her autograph book, are Derek Whyte and Alan McInally. She may keep up her affection for Celtic – according to Laraine, Vicki burst into tears when she heard on the radio that the club had won the title on the final day of the 1985-86 season – but I am not at all certain about the rest. Being the mother of three girls who need her time, Laraine has never had much time to watch Celtic play. Dawn, my middle daughter, gave her total lack of interest away when she was watching the television highlights of an Old Firm game on one occasion and asked me what colour of strip I had on! Carly, our youngest child, used to ask me every day when I came home from training if Celtic had won, so I don't think she ever really caught on in the first place!

My primary concern, which I cannot state too clearly, is that Celtic should take out extra insurance against what is happening around them. It wouldn't take too much to become an also ran in the Premier Division. Apart from Rangers, clubs like Hearts and Dundee United, because of shrewd management and wise use of their money, will gain in strength in the years to come.

The necessity is for those in control at Celtic Park to show courage now. Given the huge crowds a winning Celtic side can attract, and knowing exactly how much money that is worth, any bank worthy of the name would happily extend Celtic's credit, knowing full well they are a great risk. Who will be brave enough to set the ball rolling? Let money be used to ensure the club can hold on to its best players and more still be spent on signing others who will ensure the centenary year is a truly memorable one, and that what follows sees the club continue to speculate to accumulate. It is the only way.

History has always told the supporters that Celtic are the people's club. Let the club be given back to the people, in that case, so that they can underwrite the future. Putting your money where your mouth is ought to be taken as an honourable thing to do, and I know all about integrity in this game.

11

No Emerald Dream . . .

It will come as a shock to everyone outside of the Celtic management, because I have never revealed the story before this, to know that I was once offered the job of assistant to David Hay. If I say now that I also accepted the invitation straight away, then it will also be immediately obvious that this is one happening in my life that has to be gone into in precise detail because, whatever else I am now, it is not the assistant manager of Celtic!

In February of 1986 David Hay decided, with the full approval of the board of directors, that he had to dissolve the partnership with Frank Connor. Ironically, the break-up was carried out the day after one of the best results of what had been up till then an unsatisfactory season, when Celtic beat Dundee at Dens Park in the fourth game of a sixteen-match sequence without defeat that would carry us towards a stunning climax to the Premier Division championship three months later.

A short time afterwards the manager called me into his office and told me he felt that the two of us could work together very well for the good of the club and that he was going to put it to the board that I should become the new number two in command at Celtic Park. I was genuinely overjoyed because I had always thought, and hoped, that this would be the next logical step in my career. All of my playing life as a senior had been spent with Celtic and it would, first and foremost, have given me great pleasure to move up to a managerial position. I also felt that the chemistry I have spoken of before as an essential ingredient in such a partnership would be right between David Hay and myself. We had played together for Celtic since we were both teenagers and our temperaments were different enough, without being diametrically opposed, to make for a proper blend where the players were concerned.

David was obviously subdued by nature but I was already thinking about the coaching side of the game and I knew I would have no difficulty in telling the players under me to address me as 'boss' and not as Danny any more. That was the reason why I made up my mind that when the formal details of the transition had been arranged I would then announce my retirement from the game. To my way of thinking it had to be easier to get your point across to the players when you did not have to worry about your own game or the contribution you were making to the side, and I knew that the people at Celtic Park would accept what I had to say to them as the word of a higher authority.

After my initial discussion with the manager, David told me not to mention his proposal to anyone until it was a fact. There was to be a board meeting that night at the ground during which he would raise the subject with directors who had maintained all along that the job of running a club Celtic's size was too big for one man, in any case. I went home feeling relaxed and content but kept the good news from Laraine and the rest of my family because that had been David Hay's instruction, and trust has to be an integral part of a relationship like the one we were planning. The following day, to my amazement, the manager said nothing at all to me about the job and I knew then, instinctively, that something, somewhere had gone seriously wrong.

I was extremely angry about it, too, but my problem was that I did not know who to be angry with. It would have been better if David Hay had come up to me and apologised, even if it was only to say that he was sorry for building up my hopes unnecessarily over something that he had not thought through properly. Instead I am still in the position where I do not know to this day exactly what happened and why I did not get the job. All I can do here is present the facts as I know them and allow the people to draw their own conclusions, as I have arrived at a theory of my own.

Basically, I have to believe that the Celtic board rejected the idea of Danny McGrain becoming assistant manager. It would not make sense for David Hay to have asked me to become his partner in the morning and then change his mind later on that same day. If my assumption is correct, why, then, did the directors not want me? I cannot believe that it had anything to do with money, since the continuation of the post of assistant manager was an important issue to the board and hiring me would only have meant an increase on my player's salary for assuming the additional responsibility. So far as I was concerned I certainly had the credentials for the job in terms of experience, especially that gained under Jock Stein, Billy McNeill and the rest of the Lisbon Lions as well as a man like Jim McLean while playing for Scotland.

It has been suggested to me by the friends I eventually let in on the secret after it became obvious that the job was not mine that there is another possible explanation. That is the question of me not being a Roman Catholic. I would fervently hope that is very far from the case, given that the best manager the club ever had was a Protestant and that religion ever having anything to do with the hiring of anyone at Celtic Park would be detested by the ordinary, decent supporters of the club. I cannot accept that theory because I do not want to.

It would be some weeks in any case before I finally asked David Hay for the official reason behind my rejection, during which time I apparently contributed towards my own downfall, judging from what he told me. Celtic had started that season well but then hit the barren time that annually befalls the side because of the way they play.

What the team lacks, and has done since Billy McNeill retired as a player in 1975, is a solid, uncompromising defender who will organise those around him into a steady unit. In other words, they need to do what Rangers have done and ensure that everything is built on a secure base that does not leak, and I speak as one who was as guilty as anybody who approached 1986 in a Celtic side that lost three matches in a row to Rangers, Dundee United and Aberdeen by conceding a total of ten goals and scoring only one, and also went out of the European Cup Winners Cup in the first round at the same time. Mick McCarthy, this is your life!

There was, though, a unique explanation for that aggregate result in that Celtic had to contend with the severe drawback of taking on top-class opposition in a ground that came fully to life for European ties without the assistance of a crowd. The final part of our sentence, as imposed by U.E.F.A. over the fiasco with Rapid Vienna, was the order to play behind closed doors in the home leg of our next European tie. When the opposition was revealed as Atletico Madrid it was a punishment that could be seen to have cost Celtic a quarter of a million pounds in lost earnings from the gate as well. Celtic Park would have filled to capacity with those who remembered, or had been told about, the previous, notorious meeting between the clubs in 1974. If ever Celtic are drawn against Rapid Vienna at any time in the future, the same intensity of feeling will apply. The clamour to see the match would have been all the greater, too, after our first match against them in their own Vincente Calderon Stadium.

I, for one, could not wait to get them back in Glasgow after what happened to me with ten minutes to go of our drawn game. As I fell to the ground with one of their players, Landaburu, he deliberately struck me full on the mouth with his elbow, opening my bottom lip. As I sat in the dressing room holding an ice pack to a wound that has never properly healed, I began counting the days until we met again.

But nothing was the way it should have been when that day dawned. I have always maintained that it would be possible to be led out on to the pitch blindfolded at Celtic Park and still be able to tell it was a European match, as distinct from a domestic fixture, that was about to start. There is a feel about the place that is unlike any other occasion there. To take away the crowd is like the loss of the senses. You cannot hear the anticipation in the crowd's voices, see the look of apprehension on the other side's faces or touch the limits of your own playing ability as a result of both those incentives. I could not even pay back Landaburu because, with only each other for company, the two teams were more aware than usual of the referee's presence. No matter how many are watching, though, there ought to be a basic level of resilience and Celtic never reached it as Atletico scored a goal in each half while we had a lengthy, and unsuccessful, search for our composure.

There are times when a mild sedative in the form of a commanding figurehead would save further anguish of the sort that occurred before and after that demoralising run. Celtic went out of the Skol Cup to Hibs at Easter Road, for example, in a game that went to penalty kicks after the pair of us had shared eight goals in two hours of play. In extra time the team that scores first, which Celtic did with a marvellous goal from Roy Aitken, is expected to pay reasonable attention to the proper defence of that advantage for the remainder of the additional period. We lost yet another equaliser within sixty seconds of scoring ourselves and went out 4-3 on penalties.

At the same ground in the Scottish Cup months later Celtic's crime of omission was even greater. Having twice gained the lead, only to let Hibs equalise, we then went a goal down with only six minutes left for play when Hibs were given a penalty, from which Steve Cowan scored.

As the then holders of the Scottish Cup, our lives were just beginning to pass before our eyes when Celtic were awarded a penalty at the other end with four minutes left on the clock. Brian McClair scored and that would have been enough for any ordinary team to make sure that such time as remained passed by as uneventfully as possible. A replay against Hibs at Celtic Park would have been the equivalent of a bye into the next round, too, because there are some teams who simply cannot win big matches on certain grounds. Dundee United at Ibrox, with very infrequent exceptions, are one of them, while Hibs traditionally tend to take one look at Celtic Park and lose the will to live. That mad March day at Easter Road, though, Celtic allowed the blood that was racing by then to rush straight to our heads and went out to look for an even bigger finish in the form of a winning goal before the final whistle. It never occurred to us that Hibs might hit us back. With sixty seconds to go, Eddie May scored and knocked us out of the cup as retribution for our lack of discipline.

Because of their cavalier approach to the game a bad run of results can always be expected from a side like Celtic. It is how the storm is weathered that is the important thing. We seemed to be making no sign of a recovery at all on any front until a point was saved against Aberdeen at home that started off a long, unbeaten run that resulted in the most talked about finish to a Premier Division championship since the major league came into being.

The record books will show only the cold statistical fact that Celtic won the title on goal difference from Hearts by virtue of having scored three goals more than they did, with both sides having won, drawn and lost an identical number of matches.

Factual data will not rekindle the memory of an unforgettable last day to the league season, though. For Celtic to win by three clear goals against St. Mirren and Hearts to lose to Dundee was a fanciful looking equation for a cockeyed optimist, never mind a realist who knew that Hearts had not lost a match since the week before they had won at Celtic Park the previous October. It transpired, however, that Celtic played the best football we had managed all season and moved into a five-goal lead with thirty-five minutes of the match still to go at Love Street. The rest of the game was an eerie wait for something to happen at Dens Park.

There has been a lot of irresponsible talk since that day, implying that Celtic were lucky, or that St. Mirren were guilty of complicity by lying down and making sure that, whatever else happened, Celtic at least achieved their half of what was required to bring the title to Glasgow.

A flu epidemic among the Hearts players has also been used as excuse for their failure to hold out against Dundee, bearing in mind they conceded the goals that cost them the championship in the last seven minutes of play. Firstly, any side that goes sixteen games in a row without losing, as Celtic did, can not be damned with faint praise when all they are guilty of is coming to the top with a late flourish. There is nothing against that in the rules, so far as I know. To finish on top of the league means you were the best team in it. Next, neither St. Mirren nor any other team in the country could have lived with Celtic and the kind of form that Brian McClair and Maurice Johnston were in that day. If we had played full out for the entire ninety minutes there is no telling what the full-time score could have been. It was also a tribute to the team's collective nerve that we concentrated on what we had to do until the job was well and truly done. Hearts could not manage that and this was partly due to the professionalism of Dundee and the fresh mind and legs of someone called Albert Kidd.

When he came on as a substitute for Dundee and scored both goals, Albert was a little-known player outside the Tayside region. The revelation afterwards that he was also a dyed in the wool Celtic supporter turned him into a folk hero in certain quarters. It was all heady stuff for those who followed the club and yet for me there were mixed emotions on that incredible day. I had made up my mind that because of the disappointment over not getting the job of assistant manager at Celtic Park, and the sudden offer of a position elsewhere, the game against St. Mirren would be my last in an emerald green jersey. It should have been an astonishing farewell but I was substituted with only three minutes to go and for no good reason that I have been able to work out. I must say I would have preferred to take my bow with the rest of the players in the instant that the referee's whistle heralded the outbreak of delirium in Paisley rather than be the odd one out in a tracksuit top sitting in the dug-out.

Nothing could have spoiled the celebrations over the rest of the weekend but when I next went into Celtic Park it was, I believed, to prepare the way for my departure from the club. David Hay had called me there and told me that I was being offered a player's contract for the season that would follow.

It was then I finally cracked and asked him why I had never heard any more about becoming his assistant. The reply I was given was that the manager had changed his mind and decided he would feel more comfortable doing the job on his own. By then, of course, he had won the championship and therefore proved that, theoretically, it could be done that way. In effect, I had helped play myself out of a job. The fact remains, however, that less than a year later Celtic appointed Tommy Craig to assist David Hay and he had never even played for Celtic, which was a radical departure from tradition.

The only difference between Tommy Craig and myself that I can see, apart from that fact, is that he had by then gained an S.F.A. coaching certificate. My decision to reject David Hay's offer of new terms as a player, therefore, seemed to signal the end of my days with the club. There had been an approach made to me to go somewhere else and into the kind of job that seemed the perfect start to a new career, offering a managerial post with money to spend and an apparently glowing future assured with a club of limitless ambition. It was, however, time for me to discover once again that all is never what it seems on the surface.

12

. . . *No Diamond Life*

I had never been brought up to be free and easy with the truth, but there was a time when I found out the hard way that this otherwise character-forming lesson was not necessarily the way to go about advancing my own career. Shortly before the last game of the 1985-86 season, I was telephoned by a friend who asked me if I would consider meeting some people to discuss the idea of becoming manager of Airdrie. My experience of not getting a coaching post with Celtic had encouraged me into thinking more along the lines of a career away from the club and I thought there could be nothing wrong with meeting anyone who was interested in having me.

Jake Dalziel and his son, John, have been backing Airdrie financially for a long number of years. Jake himself is a millionaire as a result of the family's bakery business, and his dream has always been to see Airdrie playing in Europe. It was instantly very flattering and enticing to think that he considered me to be the man who could lead them there. I originally met his son, though, and was taken aback by his lifestyle. In keeping with Airdrie's nickname this was a diamond encrusted set-up with his purple Rolls Royce, complete with crest on the outside and white upholstered interior, standing in the forecourt of a beautiful home in the town of Airdrie. When he began to outline the job of Airdrie manager as he and his father envisaged it, I knew it was more than the domestic trappings that were impressive.

The proposal was that a non-repayable loan of quarter of a million pounds was to be given to the club to finance the transformation of Airdrie into a full-time side for a period of two years. This was to be the first stage of the grand design that was to lead the club into the Premier League and from there into Europe.

There was to be money made available to rebuild the main stand at Broomfield, Airdrie's ground, and an annual wage of £30,000 for the manager with a car thrown in for good measure. All of this was an offer to the board of directors at the club on one condition, namely that Danny McGrain was to be appointed in charge of team matters. When all of this was explained to me I thought it was too good to be true for a first chance at club management. I also wondered where a man with Jake Dalziel's philanthropic tendencies had been hiding, undetected, for so long in Scottish football.

It was such a good offer I set about doing my homework on Airdrie. I investigated their existing set-up behind the scenes, their scouting operation and their youth policy. On the day after Celtic won the Premier League championship at Love Street, I was a guest at the annual dinner of the Scottish Football Writers Association at a hotel in Glasgow. One of my former team-mates at Celtic Park, Dominic Sullivan, who is now the manager of Alloa, was also there with a friend of his, John McVeigh. The longer the night wore on, the more I liked the idea of John becoming my assistant at Airdrie. He was still playing in the First Division with Kilmarnock, and that was a league of which I knew nothing at all. To have a man who had played there all of his senior life to help me navigate Airdrie seemed like sound logic. As well as that, John would come to Broomfield as a player and I had already made up my mind that I would wear the club's distinctive diamond-style jersey. That way Airdrie would get two experienced players without even having to dip into the considerable fund that was there for transfers.

I might have been feeling the pace of the game week in, week out with Celtic but I also knew that my experience would get me through a season at a lower level in the league and without cheating on anyone, least of all Airdrie.

The Dalziels had been kind enough to say that getting me to come to Broomfield would be their equivalent of Graeme Souness going to Ibrox, which had happened a month before. They also assured me that there would be no other candidate beside myself for the job and it was in that relaxed, confident frame of mind that I went into my job interview with the Airdrie board.

It was on a Thursday night and earlier in the day I had refused the offer of a player's contract with Celtic, telling David Hay that I expected to be the manager of Airdrie by the following morning. I always remember his last words to me were about Celtic meeting Airdrie in the cup the following season and how he would look forward to seeing me then. I drove from the house to Airdrie's ground on my own, thinking of all the coaching ideas I had picked up over the years but had never had the chance to put into operation because quite simply, when it got to the end of a hard day's training at Celtic Park I was just too tired to do some extra work with the youngsters who would have appreciated some help. My first priority, though, was to be up to the Premier League standard of fitness and that meant conserving my energy as far as possible for a Saturday. Also, I never wanted it to look as if I was interfering with David Hay's methods unless I was invited to help out.

My horizons had been broadened, though, by working under such contrasting personalities as Jock Stein and Jim McLean at club and international level. The big man was the arch pyschologist while Jim gave the impression at times that he could actually have done with one! I had heard all the stories about how his Dundee United players were verbally abused and threatened with all sorts and I made up my mind that I would try to get the attention of the Airdrie players by some other method.

What could not be taken away from Jim, though, was his respect for fine detail. With Scotland, Jock Stein never concentrated on set pieces but Jim could keep the players interested with what we call functions, and it says an awful lot for him that after all these years that he has been manager of Dundee United his players still listen to him attentively instead of staring through the back of his head at the wall behind him.

By the time I had arrived in Jim McLean's native Lanarkshire, in any case, I was composed and looking forward to getting across my ideas to the board. My information was that the directors had met informally the previous weekend and decided that I would be returned as their unanimous choice for the post. There were nine of them in all in one small room inside the pavilion at Broomfield that is one of the landmarks of the game in Scotland and they gave me a hearing that lasted what seemed like twenty minutes.

First of all I told them that, as the new man coming in, I would like to have my own staff about me, therefore the two coaches already at the club would be surplus to requirements. This is not as callous as it sounds. The men involved had, I had discovered, lived through five previous changes of manager which made them unlucky mascots to have about the place for the next man in apart from any other considerations.

So far as the recruitment of new, young players was concerned, I expressed my alarm that Airdrie's scouts were, according to the grapevine, often to be found attending the same game together, which hardly made sense since there were three of them. This meant the net was not being cast wide enough, and in more ways than one.

It had also been brought to my attention that the local Catholic schools were not considered a suitable breeding ground for potential Airdrie players. That, I felt, would have to change straight away if only for the reason that all sectarian policies are destructive rather than constructive. No team and no manager can succeed by restricting the choice of talent available, especially when a direct competitor will accept anyone regardless of what school they attended. It was back to Jock Stein's old philosophy about always signing the Protestant for Celtic if he was given the choice between two boys of equal ability, because he knew that Rangers would not sign the Catholic. I did not want to be caught up in that trap.

Lastly I told the board that I understood their youth policy had all but been discarded. Being the product of a scheme at Celtic Park where there was continuity of promotion from youth level to the first team, I could not wait to start off youngsters who would take a pride in playing for Airdrie from an early age and who would fit into a pattern of play that would remain constant no matter which level of the club they were playing at.

The directors thanked me for outlining my plans for the future and then the man who was at that time the club's chairman, the former referee, Bobby Davidson, asked if there were any questions for me. There was only one but it was enough to take my breath away. It came from Ian McMillan, who had been a Rangers player for years and someone I had watched at Ibrox while I was still at school. Who, he wanted to know, would pay for the hold-alls if Airdrie were to start a youth team? I almost fell off my chair. Here I was on the promise of big money, a car and handsome funds to buy players who would grace a newly constructed ground that could eventually house European football and here was this man asking me where we would find the wherewithal for a few kit bags!

It was a difficult job to keep my composure. The local butcher would have been only too happy to sponsor the boys, as people do with countless amateur teams, if it was so important that Airdrie did not have to fork out. This is what I finally told Mr. McMillan. I was then ushered out of the room and told to go home and wait for the club's answer. Before leaving, though, I was also told by John Dalziel that I should come back to town later in the evening because a restaurant had been booked for a private, champagne celebration to launch my career as manager of Airdrie.

At half past eleven that night the telephone rang at my home and it was Bobby Davidson to tell me that I had been turned down for the job on a vote of five to four. I immediately called the Dalziel family but they were too upset to offer me anything other than their deepest apologies. Once again I had been left angered and embarrassed by a mysterious letdown at the last minute where a managerial position had been concerned, but this time I knew exactly where my animosity should be directed. If I had been dishonest and told the Airdrie directors what they had wanted to hear then I would probably be the manager of the club today. All the changes I had wanted to make in the first place I would have carried out irrespective of their wishes once I had assumed office. Rather than bluff my way into the job, though, I had told the truth, and in the straightforward way it had to be delivered. In the end that was what went against me.

It took me a week to get over the feeling of rejection and I think I would still be hurting yet where it not for the fact that the renewed offer of a contract with Celtic took my mind off the whole business. The Dalziel family seemed to feel almost as bad as me, since they had offered me assurances about the job that they were not ultimately able to keep. Though the family held a massive number of shares in Airdrie, my belief is that Broomfield directors subconsciously rebelled against what they took to be the idea of being railroaded into appointing me as manager.

John Dalziel invited me back out to his home to offer me his condolences in person and spoke privately of being angry enough to buy out all the directors and take over the running of the club for himself. His father, who did not keep in the best of health in the first place, had to leave the country and go to the Channel Islands for a while to get over the shock. Bobby Davidson, for his part, resigned as chairman soon afterwards, but has subsequently returned.

As for myself, I had to go back to Celtic Park and go through the potentially embarrassing situation of pretending that nothing had happened over going to Airdrie and asking if the offer of a job for another season was still available. I should make it perfectly clear that never at any time was I made to feel that I should eat humble pie. David Hay and the Celtic directors simply restored me to the family and ten days later the draw was made for the first round of the following season's Skol Cup, putting Airdrie against Celtic in Glasgow. Naturally I re-acquainted myself with all of the men who had rejected me that night at Broomfield when they came to Celtic Park for the match. The response they got from me was an extremely frosty one, and I can make no excuses for that. What could they have said that would have made me feel any better and what could I have said to them in return that would not have sounded hypocritical?

Strange as it may seem, though, the passage of time has given me back a sense of perspective over the matter. I do not resent Airdrie; in fact if they were to come back and offer me a job at some date in the future I would weigh up their approach on its merits as I would one from any other club. They very quickly got over me, though, which makes it highly unlikely our paths will ever cross again.

Within a matter of days of showing me the door they had named the man of their choice. He was a former Airdrie player and something of a hero in the town, so the appointment of Derek Whiteford was understandable, I suppose. Clear to everyone except Dumbarton, perhaps, since he had also accepted the job as their manager just two weeks earlier and had never watched the team play since taking over the role. Less than a year later he resigned, however.

Derek, though, had the credentials that were becoming impeccable for the job of manager at all levels of the senior game. He was a product of the teacher training college faculty of coaches, an S.F.A. type who had also been through their certificate course at Largs and gained the formal seal of approval. There are examples of the breed most places you look these days. Andy Roxburgh, Scotland's National Coach, is one and so is his assistant, Craig Brown. Celtic and Rangers have them, too, with Tommy Craig and Walter Smith, and there are others too numerous to mention.

I have now joined the pack on the basis that if you can't beat them you had better join them, otherwise you will never work in the game again. All experiences are instructive in some way, no matter how small, and what I went through with Airdrie taught me a number of things. Playing the establishment's game by getting the slip of paper that seems to impress so many people is one of them.

I still wonder what might have happened, if I had never been asked about hold-alls at Broomfield!

13

Wee Willie and Ally – Big Jock and Andy

Being the holder of an S.F.A. coaching certificate would appear to be like having a glowing letter of reference within the game at this present time for those who want a manager's job. But it does not give the carrier any immunity from public criticism, however. Just ask Andy Roxburgh! His elevation from the post of Scotland's National Director of Coaching to full command of the international team has been one of the most controversial decisions ever taken by the S.F.A., and they have certainly made a few in their time.

In his first year in the job, Andy Roxburgh has divided the country over his choice of players, the kind of tactics he employs and caused arguments as to what extent he has the confidence and respect of those he works with. At the very outset I would have to say I would not have given the post to Andy but I will follow that up immediately by adding that I do not think anybody else, and I include all the men I played under at international level, would have done the job any better than he has, given the identical set of circumstances.

What is clear to me, though, is that Andy Roxburgh will now stand or fall on the rate of progress that is made by certain individuals over the next couple of years. If people like Brian McClair, Ian Durrant and Derek Ferguson from Rangers and such as Kevin Gallacher at Dundee United turn their potential at international level into a realisable asset, the team manager will not only survive but flourish because he will be able to blend them into the kind of team where everyone knows instinctively what the other man is doing. If their progress is stunted, Andy is finished.

In this respect, too, Andy Roxburgh is far less fortunate than any of the illustrious former holders of the position from Tommy Docherty, Willie Ormond, Ally MacLeod, Jock Stein to Alex Ferguson, who took Scotland to her last World Cup.

All of those men were infinitely luckier for the very simple reason that they had a wealth of experience and truly international class talent at their disposal. In fairness to Andy Roxburgh, I don't think it could be reasonably said of him that he has had a disappointing start to his career as national coach because he did not know how to handle all this exceptional ability that is going about.

To my way of thinking there is only one player in the current Scotland squad who could ever be considered for selection in any mythical World Eleven and that person is Aberdeen's central defender, Willie Miller. The rest are made up of those whose careers at international level are still at the embryonic stage and others who are having difficulty in adjusting from being a good club professional to the higher grade. That is why I certainly did not blame Andy Roxburgh when he defended Graeme Souness a while ago after the Rangers manager asked not to be picked for Scotland in two European Championship matches. In fact, I would support the manager all the way on this issue and say that he should recall Souness whenever and wherever he sees fit.

The newspaper columnists and the country at large seemed to think at the time that Souness was being typically arrogant in trying to tell the national coach that he, and not Andy Roxburgh, would pick the matches in which he played — I think it was Archie Gemmill who once said that if Graeme were made of chocolate he would eat himself — but there is another side to the story. If people with Souness's length of service to Scotland are discarded in a fit of pique before they are really ready to be stood down, who do the younger element in the squad learn from? Andy Roxburgh is constructing a national side from scratch here, and he needs all the help he can get. The only mistake they made was in allowing the whole affair to become a matter for public debate. It would have been far better to devise a diplomatic cover up that would not have reflected so badly, or given such a misleading picture, where both men were concerned.

Andy Roxburgh probably has a credibility problem in that he will always run up against the hardened professionals' reluctance to take advice on how to play the game if they feel the one offering the instructions is less well qualified than they are. This was not the case with Souness but it could have looked that way. Andy's problem is that he is so young and does not have a successful club record as a manager to fall back on as a protection from the critics.

When Alex Ferguson had achieved all he could, or wanted to, with Aberdeen, I thought he was an absolute natural for the Scotland job, especially as the heir to Jock Stein, the man he so resembles in approach. Alex felt he was too young to take over that mantle, though, and yet the S.F.A. gave it to someone who was even younger still. With respect, Andy's playing career at places like Partick Thistle and Falkirk, and his work as a coach with the

Scotland Youth team, was not the kind of pedigree likely to make his settling in period a bed of roses. This is where Souness can be invaluable to him. He has an undoubted presence on the park and will be able to help all those around him. I will freely admit, too, that it is only really since I retired from the international front in 1982 that I have come to fully appreciate Graeme in a Scotland jersey.

Like the vast majority of the Scotland supporters, I was unsure of him and the contribution he made but now I can understand his full worth. For one thing he always has time on the ball when it comes to him and that is the mark of the quality player. Jock Stein could see it all in him, but that was when he had other talents to complement Souness'. Andy Roxburgh has to cling on to him, though, and allow Souness to conserve his energy for when he feels able to release it for international matches. That is why I say Jock Stein, and nobody had a greater respect for that man than I did, would not have achieved results that were any better than Andy Roxburgh's over the last twelve months, given the same basic materials to work with.

Whatever happens in the future, one thing is certain and that is Andy Roxburgh will not fail for lack of enthusiasm or improper attention to detail. In fact, there are times when I think he overdoes it and could be said to pamper the players. The idea of taking the Scotland team to the opulent splendour of the Gleneagles Hotel in Perthshire, for instance, is a move of dubious merit. And I do not say that as a veteran survivor of the bad old days in the Queen's Hotel, Largs, where a squad of players would race each other back from training because there were only three baths in the whole place and the internal plumbing system was so eccentric that all three could not be run at the same time! That was one, neglectful extreme, but taking players to this repository for the well-to-do is surely the other end of the spectrum. If the living is too easy can there be any burning desire to play a hard game of football? I would imagine that going out and, in the grand old cliché, dying for the jersey would be the last thing on your mind.

I know from personal experience, for instance, that rich food in plentiful supply is the cue for players to over-indulge and so take the edge off their fitness. It happened to a Scotland team of which I was a member before we lost a game to England at Wembley of all places. Andy Roxburgh also says that coastal resorts used by Scotland before he came along were harmful because the sea air sapped the player's energy. All I can say is that it had no harmful effect on the team's results, and staying at Seamill, on the Ayrshire coast, has done Celtic no harm over the years while excelling at home and winning the European Cup.

Maybe there is a fear of a modern-day mariner taking to sea in the dead of night for one of those pre-breakfast sails designed to work up an appetite, copyright Jimmy Johnstone enterprises, but I think the old pioneer days have gone now that we have a more sophisticated breed of player about at present.

Andy Roxburgh also has the understanding of the players in that they would not knowingly do anything to undermine his position. Roy Aitken, for example, extends that support to frequently playing in a position for Scotland that is not naturally his best, nor the one to get him the most favourable reviews afterwards. He does it, though, because he wants to see Andy Roxburgh succeed, and so should the rest of the country get behind the national coach at this time of transition. We have to persevere along with Andy while he experiments with personnel and permutations. Occasionally he has been pilloried, as when he tried to revive the days of two orthodox wingers in that match against the Republic of Ireland that Scotland lost at Hampden and discovered that nostalgia definitely wasn't all it used to be. If he has the nerve to stick to a certain team and the potential of the players in it is fulfilled, I am not one of those who would say the end is nigh for Scotland under Andy Roxburgh. He can not be one of the most respected and sought after teachers of the game in the world for nothing. If anything, Andy suffers from being different from those who have gone before him and that is why the press are having difficulty in coming to terms with him as well.

Newspapermen were spoiled by such as Tommy Docherty, the first Scotland manager I had any personal dealings with. He picked me for an Under 21 trial match at Firhill and then left me sitting in the stand the whole night without even getting a place on the substitutes bench. The Doc was always too busy thinking up his next smart remark so far as I could see and he tended to let that obscure the managerial skills he possessed.

The man who gave me my first Scotland cap was Willie Ormond, arguably the most well liked of the lot and whose record while in the job was better than anybody's. The first thing that struck me about Willie was that he was like your dad. I can still see him coming down to breakfast every morning when the Scotland team were together, gleaming like a new pin and with the smell of freshly applied vaseline in his hair.

Willie belonged to a different generation from the players and that went for the way he thought about the game, too. For all that he had been a member of the legendary Hibs forward line of the fifties that became known collectively as the Famous Five, Willie knew instinctively that he did not speak the same language as the men he had charge of two decades further on. His true forte lay in being able to spot players worthy of the international team, having the courage of his convictions to pick them and then blending them together in the best possible way. Once they got out on the park, though, it was up to the more experienced among them to exert authority.

It was Willie who brought together Jim Holton and Martin Buchan at the centre of the defence and paired me with Sandy Jardine at full back. Even though this meant moving over to the left-hand side of the field and curbing some of my attacking instincts, I was happy to play there knowing that I was helping bring something to the Scotland team that had not been there all that often, solidity. The simple efficiency he brought to the job of managing St. Johnstone stood Willie in good stead and any man who could get a provincial club like that into Europe, as he once did, had to be good at his job. Willie, though, never overplayed his hand.

Billy Bremner was his mouthpiece on the park, though there was an incident between the two of them that summed up Willie's quaint philosophy on the game just before Scotland were due to play Hungary. Leeds United, Billy's club, had met Ferencvaros, the Hungarian club side, shortly before the international and since their team contained the bulk of those to meet Scotland, he had come to Glasgow with a meticulously compiled dossier on individual players put together by Don Revie and his assistant, Les Cocker.

Willie gathered the team around him in order to thank Billy publicly for his well meaning gesture, and then threw the thing over his shoulder and into a bucket to the open mouthed, slack jawed astonishment of every onlooker. I cannot recall any team talk that lasted any longer than a couple of minutes and there were never any histrionics, even in the heat of the battle against the like of Brazil in the World Cup. Billy Bremner and Denis Law, who, like the rest of us had never played in a World Cup tie before, were physically sick with nerves even before our first match against Zaire but Willie might as well have been standing outside Muirton Park for all the difference it seemed to make to him.

But then he had Bremner and David Hay, a truly formidable player of the type that Andy Roxburgh would give anything for, I'm sure, at this particular time. Ormond came into the job as 'Willie who?' in the newspaper headlines but he came back from the World Cup in West Germany in 1974 as a national hero. Even a man with his sunny disposition aged in the job, however, and over the next three years his personality underwent a slight change as the impression gained strength that the S.F.A. wanted a new man, and one with greater charisma.

The wee man who once threw himself, fully clothed, into a swimming pool because he knew that the Scotland players, in a mood of celebration abroad, were going to duck him in the water anyway grew weary. He could sometimes be found, towards the end, sleeping at the front of the team bus on the way back from games, the burden of carrying on under trying circumstances taking its toll. Eventually, in 1977, Willie gave up the Scotland job and went off to manage Hearts rather than give his employers the satisfaction of sacking him. Once he had been carried shoulder high around Hampden to receive the acclaim of the crowd following the most important result ever achieved by the national side, the win over Czechoslovakia that took the country to their first World Cup finals.

The next man in was almost a party to having the whole team air lifted above the national stadium in a symbolic demonstration of power, presumably, prior to another World Cup. But this was to be a party thrown before any of the work had been done. The short time that Ally MacLeod was manager of Scotland seems like a dream to me now, and there were plenty of people who ultimately had good cause for wishing it was!

He came into the job with all the flair the S.F.A. could have wished for, told us we were the greatest wee nation that ever God put breath into and assured us the winning of the World Cup would be a formality on the way to achieving something better. There is no point in me claiming here that I was the one man in the country who was not with him every hypnotic step of the way. Ally had worked earthly wonders with Ayr United and Aberdeen and was, at the time of replacing Willie Ormond, the most talked about man in the country. The two people could hardly have been more diametrically opposed when it came to personality. I had never seen Ally play for Third Lanark or Hibs but he had the reputation of being an unorthodox winger. He was off beat in every respect so far as I could see.

While Willie never told you what to do on the park, because he understood you already knew better than he did, Ally never stopped telling you where you were going wrong. There was never anything amiss with the team, tactically or otherwise, once he had chosen it and a match was underway, though. If anything did have the bad manners to go wrong, he would spend the half-time break blaming the other side, the referee or even the crowd. It was never his fault or the team's. In the end that kind of blinkered thinking was his undoing, because Scotland went out of the World Cup in 1978 as a direct consequence of presuming that watching Peru and Iran, two of our sectional opponents, beforehand was a waste of time. Under Andy Roxburgh, this will never happen to any Scotland team.

People believed implicitly in Ally before the event, however, but the players began to have some misgivings when the jamboree send-off was arranged at Hampden prior to the team's departure for Argentina. At first the plan was for the entire squad to be introduced to the crowd on the park and then to soar away in a helicopter for a big finish. It was only when the astronomical cost of insuring players for that piece of aeronautical theatrics was realised, to say nothing of the safety aspect for the crowd down below, that the idea was abbreviated to the ceremony on the pitch. The players only agreed to do that much because the money raised by charging admission was going towards Hampden's restoration fund. But when we think about it now. . .!

What happened in South America once the team got there is something that can be explored in a more detailed analysis of Scotland's World Cup performances that will follow, but there was another story told to me that illustrated the widening rift that was developing between Ally and the players before a ball was kicked there. On arrival in Mendoza, where the team had made their headquarters, Manchester United's Martin Buchan, who was a complex character at the best of times and hardly a calming influence when there was unrest off the field, came storming out of his room and stalked into the foyer telling anyone who was interested that he was going straight back home again because his hotel room was too small.

Ally's way of calming troubled waters was to tell Martin that he could take his room instead, rather than telling him that if this was how he felt on the eve of representing his country in the World Cup a return ticket for one could easily be arranged. It was not the best example to set the players and discipline, as everyone now knows, deteriorated very quickly after that.

Prior to Argentina, Ally had not exactly presided over the Band of

Hope, either. There was the infamous night in Copenhagen when certain players lost all control over themselves and found that they had been banned for life from ever being honoured by their country because of it. I was there on the night the drinking and brawling took place and though I was still a complete abstainer at that time there was no sobering influence that I, or anyone else, could have exerted. One S.F.A. councillor did try to take the law into his own hands but his idea of restoring order was to take a swing at Billy Bremner, which had the effect of throwing petrol at a fire. In the atmosphere of disbelief and total lack of confidence in the national side that existed after the ignominious return from South America, the International Committee decided, in their wisdom, to turn to Jock Stein to give the team back its credibility and to reassure a disenchanted public that the days of high living and low esteem were over.

Ally MacLeod retreated into a life of privacy, but not for long. I met him at a dinner six months after the World Cup and he was as large as life and twice as unrepentant about any of it. The whole, fantasy-like, period in the international team's history might never have happened. I gave him full marks for that ability to act naturally; after all he had commited no crime. All that had happened was Scotland lost a game, drew one and won a third while the manager went into the carpet business on a part-time basis. I never denied Ally any of that mass exposure on television, either, the best known of which was his advertisement endorsing a carpet firm. Any person in his position offered a lucrative agreement like that would have done exactly what he did. If there was one exception, it would have been Jock Stein.

His image was a vital part of the reputation that travelled on before him wherever Scotland went and he guarded it jealously. When the team arrived at an airport in Ally's day or Willie Ormond's, the attention of the media was focused on Law or Bremner or Johnstone, any one of several names who were famous throughout Europe. After big Jock took over, all that stopped. This was one of the best-known managers in the world and he had such a presence about him that people were drawn to his side like a magnet.

I had started to notice it properly when we were in West Germany for the 1974 World Cup. Jock was only there as an interested observer but whenever he came to the Scotland camp the team members gathered around him as soon as he sat down to talk about football. Stein had the confidence of the players in a way that made him incomparable to others. It was a pity for him, and an even greater shame for Scotland, that he did not come into the manager's job earlier than he eventually did because I think he could have had a far stronger influence on our development at international level.

He was the identikit picture of an international manager. As a disciplinarian he was without peer. If Jock set a curfew of eleven o'clock, that was when the players came in because they knew that if they did not he would be sitting, strategically placed, in a seat that gave him a view of the front door to the hotel and the clock in the foyer. Tactically, he was on his own, but he was forced to play for a while in a more cautious way than he would have liked while regaining the interest of the public, who were suffering from a kind of flatulence brough on by being fed on a steady diet of promises the team could not keep by Jock's predecessor. His other attribute was that he could work harmoniously with the S.F.A. secretary, Ernie Walker.

That is a more complicated job than it sounds but one that has to be done for the overall good of the team. Andy Roxburgh obviously has that capacity as well, having been in the S.F.A.'s employ for many years, and being one of a long line of coaches schooled in their ways.

I have now begun the process for myself, even though it will take me until I am forty years old to be fully qualified to pass on information in their eyes. To my mind, having played the game at the highest level for a long number of years is a very specialised form of schooling as well and should not be disregarded altogether or thought an inferior type of background by people looking for a manager or coach. The reason why someone like myself did not go to the S.F.A. coaching school before this, in fact, was that, having gone through a demanding season, possibly followed by a club tour, the old Home International Series or even a World Cup, I reasoned that what I really needed was to completely recharge my batteries in the short time available to me, and as far away from other football players as possible.

I have now started my certificate course, in any case, and I'll last a lot longer than one of my former Scotland teammates who, during his first day at the coaching school in Largs, was asked to devise an exercise for a group of players and work them through it. After a couple of minutes he made some dissatisfied noises, walked straight off the training pitch and never broke stride until he had packed and gone off back to his home in England, never to return. That's players for you, though, and I have come across some characters while on my travels.

14

The World Cup

It was once said, jokingly, I think, that the reason for Scotland's failure to get anywhere was that eleven Scotsmen in the same team was just too many. Admittedly, our performances in the four successive World Cup finals for which we have qualified have often given rise to that impression but if we honestly thought there was any truth in the theory there would be absolutely no point in ever taking part in that competition again. And I don't believe the day will ever dawn when Scotland refuses to enter anything because of an inferiority complex.

If anything, our downfall over the years at World Cup level has actually been a surfeit of self belief. We think the international team only has to turn up, albeit out on its feet after a long and physically demanding season at home and having had insufficient time to prepare properly for an event of such importance, and it will be alright on the night. It is the hit or miss syndrome and there seems little likelihood of anything ever changing in the foreseeable future.

It is not, as some people think, that our level of expectation where the national side are concerned is pitched at an unrealistic level. There have been plenty of examples of countries as small as Scotland in terms of population who have produced football teams that could hold their own in any company on a global scale. They all do so, though, from a position of strength based on national co-operation, whereby the team is accommodated by the football authorities in the sense of having league schedules interrupted to help out before important matches. We, on the other hand, stagger into a possibly hostile climate worn out from a league season that is too long and without the benefit of the side playing together often enough because tight domestic schedules, governed by the need to provide fixtures for the pools companies, leave no room for practice matches.

I suspect, though, that nothing will ever change. Even if Scotland were to fail to qualify for the World Cup in Italy in 1990, a country which has had lavish enjoyment out of participating in every one since 1974 would not suffer as a consequence from a sudden drop off in spectator interest on the domestic scene. Basically, all that matters in Scotland now, so far as the crowd figures go, is that Rangers are going well. For as long as Graeme Souness is in charge of something as exceptional as the structure that has been built on enormous wealth at Ibrox, the game will prosper at the box office.

There would be a sense of loss, however, if we did not have the thrill of another World Cup to look forward to, though goodness knows we have put ourselves through some agonies in the course of competing in the ones gone by. Only the first of those, in West Germany, could have been considered something other than a trip around our own capacity for masochism. We suffered, instead, from something that is not usually numbered among our national characteristics, naivety. We went out there to take on the world by winning every single game and giving no thought whatsoever to the business of calculating how many points we would need to gain a favourable draw after the sectional stage. The bravado was muted only once and that was before and during our first match, against Zaire.

We were fortunate to get the Africans in our first ever World Cup tie, given that Brazil or Yugoslavia, who were the other countries in our group, were vastly more experienced, but there were also drawbacks. There are still those who believe that Scotland gave the game of football to the world, therefore playing one of the emergent nations should have been like doing some missionary work and instructing those less fortunate than ourselves in the finer points. The fact of the matter was that while Scotland may have held the patent for discovering and distributing football, we had given up the copyright on how to play it once the rest had taken the idea and modified it.

Zaire were not the gullible opponents they were thought to be and Scotland were also dead scared of losing to them at the same time. We knew that our opponents were technically better than ever they would be given credit for but, subconsciously, the Scotland players knew they could never tell that to the folks back home, and that anything other than a win would be greeted with ridicule and contempt. Personally, I had never felt as nervous in any match at club or international level before or after that particular game in Düsseldorf. I was only twenty-four years old, though. Denis Law, who was in the twilight of his career by then, was even worse. Just meeting Denis had been one of the most memorable things to happen to me up until then, and I can still recall the moment, too. I was outside the team's hotel in Glasgow, having arrived early because I was unsure of the routine. I could see Denis already there but I simply did not know what to say to him. Eventually he broke the ice for both of us by coming over and introducing himself to me as if we had been lifelong friends. He had been the one person I had idolised and to play in the same team as him really did mean something special to me.

We were both equals in our nervously anxious state before facing Zaire, though, and I think the relief of beating them 2-0 was so great we never stopped to consider that Brazil and Yugoslavia, who had drawn with each other in their opening match, were now tactically planning whether they wanted to finish first or second in our table after they had bettered our score against the Third-World opposition. Strategy was not for us, though. We met Brazil next, feeling like we were the best team in the world and they were subordinate to us, and there were some outstanding individual performances that night which were not amply rewarded by the final score. The look on Roberto Rivelino's face the longer the game went on, for instance, spoke a thousand words on the subject of how difficult it was to get the better of someone as uncompromising as David Hay.

A goalless draw was a farcical finish but it left us nevertheless needing to beat Yugoslavia in our final match, and here the tragic combination of circumstances which were to become familiar travelling companions on future World Cup trips befell us. Another draw was all we could get and we returned dejectedly to our dressing room only to be further devastated by the news that the last-minute goal by Brazil against Zaire had put us out of the competition on goal difference. Scotland would eventually look back on that World Cup as the team with the distinction of having been the only one not to lose a game, too.

The whole experience, a mixture of high excitement and deep frustration, should have taught us innumerable lessons that would have stood us in good stead four years later when the World Cup resumed on the continent of South America. Absorbing lessons is one thing we are no good at, however, and instead we went a very long way to court unmitigated disaster and the eventual besmirching of Scotland's good name.

The average player needs a safety valve to be released at the end of each season and the members of the Scotland World Cup squad were no different in the summer of 1978. Placing them in a hotel in Dunblane might have seemed like taking out insurance against outrageous behaviour but the fleshpots of Falkirk and Stirling are like the fleshpots of anywhere else if you are in the mood to really unwind. In some respects these small towns are even more inviting because the well-known player, who likes to have his ego flattered, is likely to be made an even bigger fuss of than normal. So it was that the discipline of the squad for Argentina was the subject of rumour, most of it well founded, long before the people involved even reached the airport to leave for South America.

Once again the team had been invested with the country's hopes, regardless of what they had heard about the manager having lost the respect of the players, and to make matters worse Scotland also came up against what was to be a recurring theme of these occasions, namely the unfortunate but all too evident sign of players having reached their peak in the preliminary stages and having nothing left to offer when the real thing started. It happened to Denis Law in 1974 and the same fate cursed Don Masson and Bruce Rioch four years later. There was no question that they had been the two most influential players in the squad leading up to the finals but they had peaked six months too soon.

In the midst of this serious discovery, which had the effect of leaving the team stranded a long way from home, there came the story that reverberated around the world and put the tin lid on Scotland's ill-starred journey. Willie Johnstone was someone I had disliked playing against when he was with Rangers. I did not know him personally but I could see that on the park his mouth was never shut and he was a perpetually gesticulating bundle of nervous energy. He could also play a fair bit, there is no denying that, either. Once we had come together for Scotland, though, I found him to be pleasant, approachable and a very down to earth man. He was almost shy, in fact, and his nervous streak always gave itself away when he was violently ill before every big international. When I heard the hastily relayed news bulletin that Willie was to be sent home in disgrace from the World Cup because he had been found to have taken an illegal stimulant after a random drugs test, I could not believe, and to this day I still cannot accept, that he knowingly did anything wrong.

The tablets he took were found to be partly made up of a banned substance, but how could he possibly have known that? And why would someone who was naturally as fast as the wind need to bother artificially improving his performance, anyway?

Besides all of that, the Scotland doctor, John Fitzsimmons, was also employed in that professional capacity by Celtic and, having known him for years, I knew he would no sooner have been a willing party to anything underhand than he would have missed mass in the morning, being a devout Catholic who went to church every day. It had to be an innocent mistake, but one which Willie Johnston, regrettably, had had to live with throughout the remainder of his playing career by enduring the taunt of 'junkie' wherever he went.

The fact is that drug taking does go on in football, but I can honestly state that I have never heard of any player operating in the Scottish League who has used barbiturates before a game. I would not like to think, either, that anyone would want to win a match so badly they would damage their health to do so, because in the end there would have to be some deterioration in performance after drug abuse. Obviously it goes on abroad, since the former West German goalkeeper Harald Schumacher has alleged that it is rife in his country and made himself a best seller in the process by making his insinuations in his biography. There is no way I could spice up this chapter of my life's story by making any such insinuations, even if I wanted to, because life on the continent is like another world to us.

The truest stimulant of the lot is scoring enough goals to beat the other side and anything other than that is not football as I know it. In all the time I was a part of the Scotland set up, the team were only once put on a special course of pills, but then the players discovered that these were to curb certain other urges while we were away from home for such a length of time!

There is, I suppose, a funny side to something like that but it is a sad indictment of some players that they cannot settle down and behave themselves when they are abroad and taking part in something as vital as the World Cup. If I were in charge of the side, I would call a meeting of all the players involved beforehand and outline exactly what code of conduct was expected of them. Essentially, all you are talking about is concentrating on football for a four-week period at most and keeping your drinking habits at a moderate level for the same length of time. If there was anyone who did not feel they could do that, they would be at liberty to make their feelings known in private and then they could be left out of the travelling party without fuss. If a person went to the World Cup and then fell by the wayside, he would be sent home immediately and the precise nature of his breach of discipline would be made known at a press conference so that the team manager, who has enough on his plate without all that nonsense, could wash his hands of the affair without any blame coming his way. If a man at the peak of his profession cannot be trusted to behave for such a short space of time, then it is a bad day for all concerned.

So far as Willie Johnston went, though, I believe a tragic mistake was made and the wonder of it was that Scotland, having slumped to bitter defeat against Peru followed by an unworthy draw with Iran, then recoverd to beat Holland. It was a typically perverse performance, of course, containing within it the goal that would ultimately be voted the best of the tournament, scored by Archie Gemmill. The Dutch possibly underestimated Scotland; after all our two previous results had given us plenty to be modest about, but it was, regardless of that, an uplifting ninety minutes. Archie's final chip over the body of Holland's goalkeeper, Jongblod, was also the abiding memory from what had been an otherwise eminently forgettable episode.

Three points from three games, which was what we managed in Argentina, is the definition of mediocrity. It also represented a high degree of embarrassment to those who had followed Scotland to another continent. The Scotland side at that time was an extension of those people's lives and I believe the players accepted and respected that. The Tartan Army, the fans' collective name, were a tremendous source of encouragement and an incorrigible breed of foot soldier. I will never forget the aftermath of one international in which I had captained Scotland against England at Wembley, when a John Robertson penalty kick had given us victory. As a country we are conditioned into thinking that anything taken from England is a blow against our oppressors and when it happens in their seat of power it really is heady stuff.

We got into our dressing room at the stadium that day making plenty of noise, therefore, only to find we had been beaten into the bath by two blokes wearing the lion rampant as dressing gowns. The team were not at all unhappy about sharing the soap with a couple of the playing public, far from it, but the Metropolitan police were less than pleased and huffily carried off our bathing companions. I don't think they were overjoyed at having been outsmarted by two men dressed as flags, since this called their powers of detection while guarding the corridors inside the tunnel into question, I suppose.

The Tartan Army disbanded in disarray at the end of the seventies, in any case, but there was an upsurge in recruitment figures again when Jock Stein assumed command of the national side. However, it was the old, unpredictable squad of players he took with him to Spain in 1982.

I freely admit now that, even though I was captain of the side, the

World Cup had come a year too late for me to turn the clock back
and have my swansong. I had known it was likely to turn out that way
sometime before we left for Spain, especially after one international
in which I had played in a full-back combination with George Burley
of Ipswich. The big man had asked us to play in a specific way
which basically meant turning ourselves into wingers who started to
go forward from deep inside our own half of the field. If the idea had
been put to me in 1974, I might just have been able to manage it
while accepting that it was such a gruelling job the man in
possession would have his international career cut short by several
years because he was burned out. By the early eighties it was
completely out of the question, however.

An inclination towards self destruction is another part of the make
up of any Scotland team, though, and we went like lemmings to the
sea in our first match against New Zealand. Newspaper photographs
had depicted their players relaxing by the swimming pool at their
hotel with a drink nearby and keeping the kind of female company
that would have had Scotland's backroom staff running for those
special pills they kept for such emergencies. When they came out on
to the park against us in Seville, the Kiwis, I have to say, looked to
me for all the world like a pub team. Scotland going three goals up
on them would not have abused anybody watching of that notion,
either, but then our fatal attraction for living dangerously came into
play.

I gave away the first goal through a combination of weariness and
the ball sticking to the studs on the sole of my boot, and when New
Zealand scored again the possibility of the ultimate humiliation did
cross my mind. Although Scotland won through in the end, I was
dropped for the game that followed, against Brazil, and so was Alan
Evans, the central defender from Aston Villa.

While that match ended in comprehensive defeat, the saving
grace of our World Cup in Spain was that Stein's Scotland team had
gone out to entertain, as eight goals in three games verified. The last
two goals were scored in a drawn game with Russia that was a
demonstration of the melodrama we take on tour every four years.
Scotland takes the lead, Scotland loses the lead with a goal that
would cause a fight among schoolboys on Glasgow Green. Scotland
equalises late on but goes out of the competition by the narrowest of
margins.

The Irish went one stage further than we did that year, and hope
springs eternally in my breast that one day in the future Scotland will
do the same. Northern Ireland have this image of being able to

create distinctions like that while all having a laugh and a Guinness, but it is clearly not as simple as that. Perhaps where they do have it over us is that they have so few players to choose from they eventually build up a close-knit, club-like atmosphere, while we kid ourselves on that Scotland has more players worthy of an international cap than there really are. Andy Roxburgh has a chance at least of constructing something like the Irish, however.

All else has failed, as the Secretary of the S.F.A., Ernie Walker, pointed out in the report he prepared, detailing his feelings on the appointment of our national coach. Writing after the team had scored one goal and taken only one point out of the 1986 World Cup in Mexico, Mr. Walker observed that, as nothing beyond the initial, sectional stages had ever been achieved by Scotland while under the management of men like Willie Ormond, Ally MacLeod, Jock Stein and Alex Ferguson, all men with distinguished records at club level, the S.F.A. felt justified in taking a new direction with Andy Roxburgh. He could be right, so long as we face up to the truth at the outset.

Andy is dealing with the best of a bad bunch so far as players are concerned and the team, as yet, has no discernible pattern of play. Anybody who disagrees with either of those statements is not being honest with themselves. Where Scotland could get lucky, though, is that with the majority of those who are available just now being young enough to stay intact as a team until the next World Cup finals, and even beyond, there will not be a problem of getting there and finding that some have gone over the hill while making the journey. If that nucleus can be added to by the discovery of some bright, young talent over the next three years, Scotland will re-enter the fray as optimistically as ever. The hard part, though, will be getting there in the first place.

There will be no help from the game's administrators because domestic football, with most of the clubs dependent on the earnings from the pools companies, will not allow league football to be disrupted for the benefit of the national side. Andy Roxburgh's preparation will, we can guarantee, be first rate, but it will be of paramount importance that the team has some semblance of a playing style worked out as well. It is supposed to be a team game but Scotland has always relied heavily on individual expression, and at the moment there is a dearth of quality players available on the scale of a Billy Bremner, Sandy Jardine or Kenny Dalglish to provide it.

I could, though, pick you an imaginary side, drawn from all the

Scottish internationalists I played with between 1973 and 1982, that would not do too badly. If it is any encouragement to Andy Roxburgh, I would choose among them four of the current players whom he could rely on to get Scotland to Italy in 1990. In goal I would have Aberdeen's Jim Leighton just in front of the old Leeds favourite, David Harvey. My back four would, with all due modesty, have Sandy Jardine and myself at full back. Many people were kind enough to say we were the best combination Scotland ever produced in those areas and it would be impolite to disagree with that! In central defence, Alex McLeish and Willie Miller were, and still are, a great partnership.

Billy Bremner and Graeme Souness would be in my midfield for the obvious qualities of determination and solid use of the ball they would bring to that quarter, and I would complement the pair of them by adding Bruce Rioch. Bruce had a military bearing about him as well as an English accent that would have made him unintelligible to the vast majority of the Scotland supporters, but I have never met a man who took such a pride in playing for his country or who thought so deeply about the game. He was often my room mate on international trips and a more civilised person you could not wish to meet.

Up front I must start with Kenny Dalglish. He took a while to get started in a Scotland jersey, which might entitle Andy Roxburgh to think that those being criticised now will one day be applauded in his team, but who could argue with what Kenny has achieved? Joe Jordan, by the same token, may not be everyone's vision of how the game should look but he got results, and if it is finesse you are after I would finish off my team by giving a place to Davie Cooper of Rangers in front of John Robertson from his Nottingham Forest days, and, believe me, that makes Davie Cooper some player.

Those eleven Scotsmen in one team would have been enough for anybody who was on our side, and only too much for the opposition.

15

Reflections

Looking back on twenty years with Celtic and on my time as a Scotland internationalist, I have absolutely no regrets about anything that I did, or anything that happened to me. To have misgivings would be to feel that I had missed something and I am not the type to dwell on what might have been. I am only too happy to have had a what was! It is for others to say, as they have done, that not getting to the 1978 World Cup finals in Argentina, for instance, must have been a bitter disappointment because I was deprived of the chance to test my skills to the limit and see if that made me the best full back on the face of the earth. I don't believe that I would have made one scrap of difference to anything that came Scotland's way and for the very simple reason that I did not play in the type of position on the park where I could exert an influence that strong on the rest of the team. Also, it is always the ones who are not there on occasions such as that who end up with their reputations enhanced. It's the easiest get out clause covering the biggest tournament in the world.

Being a realist, I am only concerned with things I have some control over. The way I left Celtic Park should have been one of those and since that right was taken away from me when I was given a free transfer I have to be completely honest and say that I can not truthfully wish the club's directorate all the best for the future. I did not even shake David Hay by the hand on the day that I will always remember as the worst of my life, May 12, 1987, the day I walked out of Celtic Park because I was no longer wanted.

In spite of having been put in my place when Tommy Craig was appointed assistant manager of the club ahead of me, and when I had been offered the job first, I still clung to the hope that a post would be given to me inside Celtic Park. Helping look after the reserve team would have been enough, but it was the final insult to be told it was thought I had insufficient experience. After two decades of cups, caps and championships!

Playing for Celtic meant something to me and yet I was deprived even of the opportunity to stage a public demonstration of my affection for the supporters who had willed me back to full fitness after so many setbacks with injury and illness. On the night before

127

David Hay told me he was letting me go, one of the club's most fervent fans, who had invited me to his wedding a year earlier, telephoned me to say he was naming his son, born that day, Danny after me. These were the people who mattered to me. Had I known my last ever game at Celtic Park would be the one that was played against Falkirk ten days before I was released, I would have liked to have gone out on to the centre of the field and waved goodbye. I am surprised Celtic did not see the commercial prospects in that, in fact, because it might have put more on to the gate and the club rarely turns its nose up at a few extra pounds.

The record books will also show that the 650th, and last, time Danny McGrain ran out in a hooped jersey was at Tynecastle against Hearts. I am angry nobody ever told me that was to be my swan-song for two reasons. The first is that my father and mother never bothered to go to Edinburgh that day, thinking there would be another season with Celtic for me, so they missed out on an experience that would have been of sentimental value to all of us. What also annoys me is that the police insisted the Celtic players go out and salute the supporters at time up that day because they were refusing to leave the ground otherwise. But I did not go because I was so embarrassed at the team having lost for the second week running, and on the day that Rangers were receiving the Premier Championship trophy at Ibrox. Now the chance will never arise again.

Later on that same night, I was a guest of honour, too, at the Danny McGrain Celtic Supporters club in Stirling. To think about it all is, even now, hard to take.

I did ask David Hay why he had not told me sooner so that I could not only have come to terms with being freed by Celtic but also gone out with a flourish. His reply was that he did not want the business to affect my game, which is a staggering comment to make to someone my age. Perhaps that is partly why I am so keen on management, so that I can handle players in a way I think they should be treated, whether it is giving greater respect to someone who is nearing the end of his career and is looking to make a dignified exit or having something to do with shaping the next generation of players, and before it is too late in some cases.

'Burn out' is a term that originated within the game of tennis and was used to describe the physical damage done by young players who took too much out of themselves by taking part in too many matches before their bodies could properly withstand that kind of pummeling. In Scottish football today there is a danger of that principle working in reverse, with some players having their careers prematurely ended because they have done so little hard work in their formative years and do not have the stamina to last the pace. I am serious when I say that with the way they lead their private lives now, there are some who will not last beyond the age of twenty-five playing in the Premier League.

For anyone reading this who thinks these are the words of a 37 year old man who has had his day and can neither stand the thought of, nor fully understand, the new breed, I need only offer some names of character witnesses from my own age group as an illustration of my argument. Kenny Dalglish, Sandy Jardine and Graeme Souness will not see thirty again unless it is on the front of a bus in Liverpool, Edinburgh or Glasgow, yet they are still making outstanding contributions at their clubs because they looked after their health at the time when they had to, which was in their younger days.

When Frank Connor was assistant manager at Celtic Park he had an expression that he would use to the teenage element there about putting something in the bank for later. I knew exactly what he meant. The modern day player, for example, sees nothing wrong with going straight from the park to the pub on a Saturday night after the game. In fact, no matter how young he is, he would be thought unusual if he did not follow the standard practice. They are not there, either, to sip a soft drink or get daring on a shandy. How can that be right? Because they are professional footballers, they don't believe they will ever suffer, physically, either from the ravages of drink or anything else they get up to.

Some of them might even try to tell you that they need that Saturday night break away from the pressures in the game. I have been in this business a long time and I would like to know where you find this pressure they are always on about. So far as I was concerned, the hard part was working at training all week. On a Saturday you get the day off for a game of football, if you ask me. Pressure might be what the bloke on the terracing is suffering from if he is unemployed and has a wife and family to bring up. It should not apply to supposedly healthy young men earning good, steady money.

I would not like it to be thought I was born with a scowl on my face and a mean spirit; we are talking, after all, about a veteran of the Largs regatta for sailors without oars in 1974, but times have changed and a stricter form of management is definitely required. When I was just into the first team at Celtic Park, Jock Stein was a great believer in getting his players married off as young as possible. A happily domesticated man was a contented part of the side in the big man's book and he was delighted to hear I had been going out with the same girl since I went to school.

He might not have been so cheerful if he'd known that I used to walk home from Laraine's house to my own sometimes and once stumbled blindly into a duck pond while taking a short cut through a park in the middle of a snowstorm, but we have been together since we were seventeen because Laraine could not resist people who played for Maryhill Juniors and the marriage contract was the best one I ever signed. People in general tended to marry at a younger age in those days, though, but not so now.

That is probably a pity because the other good thing about the settled life was that it presented a more down to earth base where the player was less likely to get carried away by his own progress in the team. It is a fundamental necessity that you have someone about you who is totally honest with you about your play besides yourself. My father came to watch me almost everywhere I played with Celtic but in spite of the fact that he had played the game himself he never once tried to criticise me. By nature, he was just too soft. But then I had a 'foster parent' at Celtic Park. If ever there was anything I, or anybody else, wanted to know about anything from personal performance to the length of your hair, big Jock had an opinion on it and was never shy to come forward and tell you exactly what it was.

I have sat in dressing rooms recently, though, and listened to plenty of players demonstrating their capacity for self delusion. It was not the fault of whoever first had the journalistic idea of introducing stars for merit at the end of football reports, but that person nevertheless has a lot to answer for. The Monday morning after the match can seriously be taken up with a debate on how many stars each individual got and this can actually have the effect of making some players believe they had a better game than they really did, and run away with the idea that they are better players than they really are.

The sporting press in this country has made certain people legends in their own minds but I do not hold that against the journalists themselves. If a person is vain enough to believe everything that is written about them, to the extent that they can no longer differentiate between their own personality and the one that has been created for them because they happened to have a fine weekend on the park and got a good report in the Sunday papers followed by a feature piece on the Monday morning, then that is their fault. I have to be totally predictable in one sense, however, and say that I am one of those who has yet to read an account of a match in which I have taken part and found it to be an accurate summing up of the same game I was at! Maybe it is the angle from which the men in the press box see the play as opposed to those who are down in the park. By and large I certainly could not be critical of the sports writing fraternity, though. They successfully created for me what could only be described as a goodie-goodie image over the years.

I was never the type to court publicity but I was given the character of an honest to goodness family man and I am duly grateful for that. It will certainly do me no harm in future if parents think they can send their sons to whatever club Danny McGrain is associated with and know that their offspring will be instilled with what are regarded as worthwhile values.

The other side of the page, so to speak, is the way in which prominent footballers can sometimes have their private lives invaded by other reporters who interfere in matters which are not the public's concern. I had first-hand experience of this while I was coming to terms with being a diabetic and trying to keep my illness strictly confidential. I had set myself the task of getting over the fear of diabetes and convincing myself that I could lead an undisturbed life as a Celtic player, but it had to be done without an audience looking on.

How the story got out that I was a diabetic I do not know. One day, though, I was taking our family dog for a walk near the house when I became aware of a car trailing me as I moved down the street. One of the occupants was a reporter from a Sunday newspaper who asked me outright if it was true I was a diabetic. I never even broke stride because I did not want to answer his questions on the basis that it was none of his business. When I got back home, Laraine told me she had been interrogated first of all. It is not difficult for a player to use his contacts and find out what is going on, and once I learned the story of my medical condition was to be printed in any case it meant I had to alert some members of my family who had not been told in case it worried them. This included telephoning my middle brother, Robert, in New Zealand before the Scottish newspapers reached him and he began to worry unduly that his children might be affected by diabetes. This is an exteme example of how publicity can affect people in the public eye in an unforeseen way.

I often wonder, though, if the players obsessed by their press cuttings ever go into a room of their own, as I have done after a match, and use it as a one-man confessional to own up to themselves about just how well they really have done. No matter how good anybody else tells you that you were, only the player knows the truth deep down.

The trouble is that very few of them actually think about the game to any passable degree in this day and age. They know that they will have to play in a certain style on the Saturday to nullify the opposition and that is all they care about. In the twenty years that I played the game at the highest level it gradually became technically more sophisticated but that meant growing increasingly boring as well.

In saying that, I freely admit that if I were to take charge of a club I would need to conform to the way the game is played now or else become a revolutionary manager on the dole, but I would still like to think that I would have the nerve to introduce a few ideas of my own for making the players at my club aware of what was going on around them. For a start, I would not be afraid to give the really young ones written homework to do. The trend now is to do anything in the afternoon except discuss your work, but I would not get any job satisfaction if I did not think that those under my care were taking in what they were being told. I would have pre-arranged numbers given to set pieces, for example.

You know that wonderful moment when the team lines up to take an elaborately rehearsed free kick as the crowd draw breath in expectation of something stunning happening, and then the players hunched over the ball run in opposite directions and nobody ends up kicking it. That should never be allowed to happen unless it is to re-create the old one Aberdeen used to perfection, where the free kick was deliberately fluffed to make the other team momentarily relax before someone floored you with what they had intended to do all along. And it would not happen, either, if the players had what the American coaches in the gridiron game of football call game plans. On a given signal, all the players on one side ought to know what is going on at a set piece and the other team should be dry in the mouth wondering how they are going to be caught out by the element of surprise.

I can see nothing wrong, either, with players being told to look the part. Once again, I have had my hair permed and grown beards with the best of them, but what I am talking about is putting players in a smart club outfit that gives them a strong sense of identity. It was one of the first changes that Graeme Souness made at Ibrox and no-one could say that he lacks a certain style or is out of touch with the modern world.

Where Graeme might fall down, though, is on the question of discipline on the field of play. He was sent off twice in his first season as Rangers' player/manager and attempted to divert attention away from himself by saying that other players had conspired to get him dismissed. That is complete nonsense, and I would be the last one to say that referees are always right and players are wrong. A more cynical type of professional player certainly does now populate the game, one who would try to get his fellow professional sent off by feigning injury, but I think Graeme would fall short on witnesses to corroborate his story on the occasions he has been involved.

He and other managers could help the sport in general now, in fact, by showing greater integrity and insisting on the same from the men at their disposal. There are two main types of field offences these days: one is the opponent who tries to con the referee by writhing about on the ground after any form of physical contact. Latterly, when I played for Celtic, I would come off the park being prepared to absolve referees from blame where this type of thing was concerned. That is because it struck me that most of them could not have been around when tackling came into the category of being hard but fair and when the person challenged did not immediately think of trying to get the other side reduced to ten men. The longer it goes on, though, the more referees should do themselves a favour and cut down on it happening by booking offenders for wasting everybody's time, a kind of contempt of court for habitual criminals.

The other, even more contemptible offence is the high incidence of people who knowingly try to inflict serious injury on fellow players by use of their elbows or heads. Someday one of those elbows that have opened up countless noses and split innumerable lips will strike a windpipe and cause sorry damage, as will the defenders who connect heads in a premeditated way with forwards inside the penalty area at moments of danger.

In these instances the referee has my every sympathy because there is so much going on that is hidden or deceptive he can only catch what the human eye can see. Having been connected with Celtic for so many years, I am well aware that the club's supporters felt that what the referees could see best was everything for the other team and nothing but bad in the side wearing green and white hoops. Believing in dark plots against any team is not one of my failings, though, and I especially choose not to accept that any man goes out to ensure one side shall win and the other shall lose. We have only to look back on the evidence of the first game in which Graeme Souness actually played for Rangers against Celtic when we were awarded two penalty kicks within minutes of each other, gained a third goal that came into the doubtful category where its legality was concerned and also saw the Rangers manager booked in between. Was that not enough to get paranoia a bad name, particularly when the referee involved was Bob Valentine, from Dundee, a man that David Hay had once said should never be allowed to take charge of a game in which Celtic were playing because of doubts about his ability to be impartial?

The only referee I was ever personally wary of was Andrew Waddell of Edinburgh. I think he must have booked me in every Celtic game he had charge of and he was also the one who sent me off for the one and only time in my career. That same day he called Billy McNeill, now back as Celtic's manager, out of the dugout and publicly lectured him in front of a huge and sensitive crowd, angered by his decisions. The two of them stood eyeball to eyeball in the way heavyweight boxers do in the middle of the ring before the first bell goes to start the contest, and unless everyone was very much mistaken Mr. Waddell seemed to be quite enjoying the attention.

Personalities aside, I am all in favour of law and order on the field with a stronger commitment to discipline off it. So far as the young players are concerned I wish they would stop to think of how many of the boys who played beside them in their school team ever made it much beyond that grade of football. At the very outset of my working life I realised that the talent I had for playing the game was going to buy me my release from worrying about finding a job, earning a living and supporting a family. Surely now that the unemployment situation in this country has, regrettably, become much worse in the twenty years that have passed since then, those who are given the opportunity with a prominent senior club should grab it with both hands and pay proper attention to their work as well.

Loyalty to one particular club ought to be a reciprocal arrangement, of course, but that, as I have found out, need not always be the case. The rewards in between starting and finishing can be substantial, though. Enough, I would have thought, to make the straight and narrow the best road to take.

16

The Future

Life, as someone once said, is what happens to you while you are busy planning something else. I had not legislated for leaving Celtic Park after twenty years there but now that one very long chapter of my life has been brought to a close for me I have to think about what I am going to do with myself next. The first thing is to break the habit of saying 'we' when I mean Celtic. If it has been taken from reading between the lines of this book that I am bitterly disappointed with how my career with Celtic was brought to a close, then I cannot deny this is the case.

A few days after I was given my free transfer by David Hay, I met the chairman of the club, Jack McGinn, at the annual dinner of the Scottish Professional Footballers' Association. He told me how disappointed he had been on a personal level to read my account of how Celtic had handled my release. When I expressed surprise that he should feel that way, Mr. McGinn said it was because he had no knowledge of the club's decision to let me go until he saw it in his morning newspaper. In other words, it was nothing to do with him. That, for me, was the last straw. I had always understood that management and directorate got together to discuss who was going and who was staying at any club when the season had come to an end, particularly someone who had been there longer than the chairman and the manager. The whole business was a devastating experience for me in that I was offloaded without any semblance of dignity after two decades of what I had thought was meritorious service to Celtic. Since the day and hour I walked out of the park as an ex-Celtic player, I have never returned to the place, and the way I feel at the moment that could be a permanent condition unless I come back as part of another club involved in playing a game there.

I even arranged to have my boots and passport sent out to my home from Celtic Park rather than go through the pain of revisiting the ground to collect them. It is terrible, I know, that a man of my age and experience should harbour these feelings but I only speak my mind because I felt so close to the team and the supporters for all of those twenty years with Celtic. I could hardly bring myself to attend a dinner in honour of the European Cup-winning team, the

Lisbon Lions, on the twentieth anniversary of the club's finest hour, which also happened to be the same month that I signed for Jock Stein and Sean Fallon. To be among the fans who wanted to say a personal farewell to me on the night was, I found, emotionally overwhelming. This is the eve of the club's centenary year as well but in my present frame of mind I do not know if I could force myself to take part in any of the celebrations.

Let there be absolutely no doubt that I wish the team every success in the future, because I have nothing against the players, either individually or collectively, but I cannot say the same thing for the men who run the club. Perhaps I will be able to come back with a different attitude if things change behind the scenes at Celtic Park.

If my oldest daughter, Vicki, wants to keep up her support for the team, I will have no objections but I will ask her favourite player, Alan McInally, to get her a ticket and ask somebody else to take her. I am now in the world outside Celtic Park and trying to keep up my association with the game. There was never any likelihood of me giving up the playing side because the day has not yet dawned when I have wakened up and felt it was too much for me to go on, and I need to know within myself when that day arrives. It would be awful for me to retire with a nagging suspicion that I could have played on for a while longer.

It is definitely not a case of the battle-scarred old veteran unable to admit defeat. There are things I still have to do, examinations I have yet to set myself, even at the age of thirty-seven. Playing a leisurely game of golf on a Saturday afternoon is no use to me. I am a fairweather player of the game, and you know how often we get fair weather in this country. I have no recreational pastimes other than football and I am more than willing to put on the line a good name that took twenty years to build up. The thought of failing cannot even enter my head because I believe young players will listen to me and give me respect, knowing that I have been through it all.

This will also enable me to get over the essential differences between being with one of Britain's biggest clubs, Celtic, and one from a lower division. Obviously I will not, in the main, be mixing with the players who have the same ability, or time and energy to devote to developing their skills, as I left behind. The basic enthusiasm of the average part-time player may not be as great, either, and if it is not, then I cannot instil it in them. What I can do, though, is work very hard on those who do want to get on, and that will also include the schoolchildren it is my intention to coach under a special scheme. With the help of a sponsor, I intend setting up my own coaching clinics in centres around Scotland in 1988.

This would involve boys coming along to be instructed by myself as well as getting visits from guest players and days of studying from video films. Visits to the local senior ground would also be included so that the boys could go away at the end of their week with a fully comprehensive picture of what it takes to become a worthwhile professional in terms of hard work and discipline.

It is my contention that the well-known name will be more readily listened to than a school teacher or boys' club leader. At one time I used to blame the school authorities for not opening their doors and letting the professional in to train the youngsters but I now think this is a better way of doing it, in any case. It will be a more demanding game at the highest professional level in the next five years, and only the fittest will survive, as well as those who are hungriest to get on. You could sum up my attitude to the question of temperament by saying you can take the boy out of Drumchapel but you can't take Drumchapel out of the boy. I would like to see my summertime coaching clinics, and the club I'm with, have a backbone of kids from the Glasgow housing schemes. These are the people who will fight the hardest for you when the chips are down. There is also more to life than being connected with a well-run boys' club, of which there are hundreds today, and being beautifully kitted out with a sponsored strip as well as a display cabinet full of medals at home that do not really signify anything.

I have stood on the touchline with friends of mine at games like these, and from what I can gather it is a collection of parents all shouting for their individual child. There is nothing at all wrong with that kind of family support but it is not teaching the boys very much about the value of teamwork, which is where the time-served professional could be of use. If I, or anybody else like me, visited a school to work, though, there could be a problem after we had gone and the long-suffering teacher had to re-assert himself while trying to run the team.

If a full breakdown on what it takes to play with a Premier League club, and the good habits it entails, takes kids off the streets and saves them roaming into vandalism, violence or abusing their own bodies with drink or drugs, then so much the better. And the first thing they will require is the heart to go right to the very top, the willingness and courageousness to be first to the ball and to be unafraid of going in where it might hurt to get it.

The difference between being hard and being dirty also has to be emphasised. I came from a club where to deliberately injure an opponent was the lowest form of human behaviour and where the culprit was fined or put out of the side as punishment, be it first team or reserves. We have the talent in abundance in this country, always have had, always will, but it is how it is harnessed that is the crucial factor. One of Celtic's problems in recent years, in fact, has been the noticeable lack of good youngsters breaking through from the second team, and here the club could do themselves a favour by upgrading their own training facilities and not hampering such potential talent as exists at Celtic Park.

When Billy McNeill was first manager of the club he wanted to take Celtic away from Barrowfield, the side's training pitch near the ground, to a custom-built complex that would have been for our exclusive use and where there was space for office premises as well as a canteen for the players. The directors, so far as I understand, objected to the cost of this venture and a good idea was lost because Barrowfield is, in my opinion, totally unsuitable for a club of Celtic's standing. It is not completely closed off, for one thing, and that is how the players arrived one day to find someone on a motor bike racing all over the ground on which we were supposed to practise our basic skills. If, in spite of the fact that his tyre tracks could have badly injured an important player, there is at least an element of humour about that incident. It was not so funny on the day that one of the poor, unfortunate youngsters from the surrounding area wandered dreamily on to the training field still clutching the bag from which he had just been sniffing glue.

Apart from due care being taken with training, scouting has also become an important job at any club in an era in which Rangers have created a climate whereby clubs are willing to pay big money for success in the short term while hoping that their own handpicked youths will take care of the future.

This is now something that I will have to learn to do for myself because I have only been used to the very best players reaching their creative peaks in front of big crowds. The first time I watched a match involving two teams from a lower division, I could not separate one player from another in my own mind. So far as ability was concerned, they all looked alike to me. This should not be misconstrued as a disparaging remark, it is simply meant to amount to a confession of personal vulnerability in that direction. I am prepared to devote the rest of my working life to what it takes to become a first-class manager, though, because I am more afraid of not getting the chance to put into practice all the ideas I have, and seeing if they work, than I am of falling on my well publicised face.

It is, after all, not my reputation as a player that is under private and public scrutiny but my ability to judge good from bad and my technical capabilities for outmanoeuvring the other man. That will all be tested on the first rung, and hopefully there will be other steps to be taken in an upward direction after that. I honestly believe that if I put in the same percentage of effort and hard work that I did for Celtic, then I will pull through the sphere of management.

If I did not have that unshakeable confidence in my own ability, I would be off in the opposite direction to live in peace with my press cuttings. But I do not want to be remembered as the one who fractured his skull and then got even more sympathy because it was discovered he was a diabetic as well. For the sake of my own peace of mind, I need to have the chance to find out if what I know is relevant to the game in its present, continuing state of flux.

Within the next five years I think we will have the first organised British Cup, or league tournament set along those lines and only concerning the very best. If the English clubs are still barred from taking part in any of the European competitions by then, there could be as many Englishmen playing for the Scottish clubs as anything else. I want to be immersed in all that excitement somewhere.

If I am not and the reason for that is my failure elsewhere in the interim, I will not look for others to blame. That was not the way the late Jock Stein brought me up in this game. I will take the criticism or the praise if it is due to me. My overriding concern is that I get the chance to see which one it is eventually. I feel I am due that much because of the experience I have to offer. Management is, I appreciate, one profession that carries with it no promise of job security. If Jock Stein can be removed from Celtic Park, when he was, historically, the club's outstanding figure, then anything can happen. I am prepared to take the rough with the smooth, though, and to continue living my life in sunshine or in shadow.

All the Facts

Born in Glasgow on 1st May 1950. Schoolboy football at Camus Place Primary, Drumchapel, and Kingsridge Secondary, Drumchapel (Scottish Schoolboy internationalist); Queen's Park Victoria X1; Celtic apprentice professional farmed out to Maryhill Juniors before signing as a professional in 1967.

Honours with Celtic
League championship medals: 1973, 1974, 1977, 1979, 1981, 1982, 1986 (7)
Scottish Cup: winners medals in 1974, 1975, 1977, 1980, 1985 (5), finalist in 1973, 1984 (2)
League Cup: winners medals in 1974/75, 1982/3 (2), finalist in 1972/73, 1973/4, 1975/6, 1976/77, 1983/84 (5)

Appearances (major competitions only), excluding substitutions

	League	League Cup	Scottish Cup	European comp.	Totals
1970/71	7	4	—	1 (EC)	12
1971/72	2	4	1	2 (EC)	9
1972/73	30	10	7	4 (EC)	51
1973/74	29 (1)	13	3	5 (EC)	50 (1)
1974/75	30	7	5	2 (EC)	44
1975/76	35	9 (1)	1	6 (ECWC)	51 (1)
1976/77	36	10 (1)	7	2 (UEFA)	55 (1)
1977/78	7	2	—	2 (EC)	11
1978/79	18 (2)	1	4	—	23 (2)
1979/80	34	6	6	6 (EC)	52
1980/81	33	8	3	4 (ECWC)	48
1981/82	27	5	2 (1)	1 (EC)	35 (1)
1982/83	33 (1)	10 (1)	3	4 (EC)	50 (2)
1983/84	33	10	5	6 (UEFA)	54
1984/85	30	3	7	4 (ECWC)	44
1985/86	27	2	2	2 (ECWC)	33
1986/87	21	1	4	2 (EC)	28
	432 (4)	105 (3)	60 (1)	53	650 (8)

N.B. Excludes appearances as a substitute. Figures in brackets are goals scored.

Abbreviations: EC — European (Champions) Cup
ECWC — European Cup-Winners Cup
UEFA — UEFA Cup

International appearances

Scottish Schoolboy internationalist. Scottish under-23 internationalist (2 appearances).

'Capped' 62 times for Scotland at full international level. Holds club record for number of international appearances (i.e. when with club):-

1973 v. Wales, N. Ireland, England, Switzerland, Brazil, W. Germany, Czechoslovakia (2).
First 'capped' v. Wales at Wrexham on May 12th 1973 (Scotland won 2-0).

1974 v. Wales (sub.), England, Belgium, Norway, Zaire (WCF), Brazil (WCF), Yugoslavia (WCF).

1975 v. Spain, Sweden, Portugal, Wales, N. Ireland, England, Rumania, Denmark (2).

1976 v. Switzerland, N. Ireland, England, Finland, Wales (2), Czechoslovakia.

1977 v. Sweden, Wales, N. Ireland, England, Chile, Argentina, Brazil, East Germany, Czechoslovakia.

1979 v. Belgium.

1980 v. Portugal (2), N. Ireland, Wales, England, Poland, Hungary, Sweden.

1981 v. Wales (sub.), England, N. Ireland (2), Israel (2), Sweden.

1982 v. Holland, Spain, N. Ireland, England, New Zealand (WCF), U.S.S.R. (WCF — sub.).
Last 'capped' against U.S.S.R. (Russia) in World Cup finals match at Malaga, Spain, on June 22nd 1982. Came on as substitute for Strachan in 70th minute of match, which ended 2-2.

N.B.   WCF — World Cup finals. 1974 in West Germany, 1982 in Spain.
Dates refer to years in which matches played, not season.

Awards

Scottish Football Writers Association 'Player of the Year' of season 1976/77.
M.B.E. (New Year's honours list, 1983).

Index